Ministerial Barrenness

Dag Heward-Mills

Parchment House

Unless otherwise stated, all Scripture quotations are taken from the King James Version of the Bible.

MINISTERIAL BARRENNESS

Copyright © 2022 Dag Heward-Mills

First published 2022 by Parchment House

[77]Find out more about Dag Heward-Mills at:

Healing Jesus Campaign
Email: evangelist@daghewardmills.org
Website: www.daghewardmills.org
Facebook: Dag Heward-Mills
Twitter: @EvangelistDag

ISBN : 978-1-64330-622-3

Contents

CHAPTER 1

Barrenness in Ministry

SING, O BARREN, THOU THAT DIDST NOT BEAR; break forth into singing, and cry aloud, thou that didst not travail with child: for more are the children of the desolate than the children of the married wife, saith the LORD.

Enlarge the place of thy tent, and let them stretch forth the curtains of thine habitations: spare not, lengthen thy cords, and strengthen thy stakes; For thou shalt break forth on the right hand and on the left; and thy seed shall inherit the Gentiles, and make the desolate cities to be inhabited.

Fear not; for thou shalt not be ashamed: neither be thou confounded; for thou shalt not be put to shame: for thou shalt forget the shame of thy youth, and shalt not remember the reproach of thy widowhood any more. For thy Maker is thine husband; the LORD of hosts is his name; and thy Redeemer the Holy One of Israel; The God of the whole earth shall he be called. For the LORD hath called thee as a woman forsaken and grieved in spirit, and a wife of youth, when thou wast refused, saith thy God.

For a small moment have I forsaken thee; but with great mercies will I gather thee. In a little wrath I hid my face from thee for a moment; but with everlasting kindness will I have mercy on thee, saith the LORD thy Redeemer.

Isaiah 54:1-8

I am writing this book to help you to break out of barrenness in your ministry. Barrenness is a terrible, depressing and devastating problem that happens both in the natural and in the ministry.

Barrenness in ministry is the cause of much of our discouragement, disappointment and disillusionment. I once read a book in which the reasons for the fall and destruction of pastors were outlined. Among the top causes of pastoral failure was discouragement. Many pastors fall out of the race through discouragement and disillusionment. I can tell you that when you become fruitful, you will not have the chance to be discouraged or disillusioned. The fruits you have borne will keep you busy and will give you joy. How joyful a woman is when she brings forth a child!

O what a joy it is to become fruitful in God!

Lots of knowledge without fruitfulness is nothing! The kingdom of God is more than a school of history and doctrines. There is more to ministry than the acquiring of numerous certificates of Bible knowledge. Have you noticed that some of the most learned and scholarly Bible expositors are very ineffective at real ministry? In fact, sometimes the more scholarly they become, the more faithless, godless and barren they are.

Bearing fruit is a very spiritual thing. Have you wondered at the immense fruit that Christ Jesus bore? Over two thousand years have gone by and He has more fruit than He has ever had before!

Barrenness is the reason for the lack of real fruit in the modern Christian church. There are a lot of activities and a lot of programmes but there is little or no fruit. Some pastors are barren. No matter what they do, their ministries never flourish. When the spirit of barrenness is taken away you break out in fruitfulness.

God wants us to be fruitful. God wants us to expand in ministry. In order to be fruitful you must understand what barrenness really is. Barrenness is a problem that God wants to deal with in your ministry.

In the next few chapters, we will be studying the concept of spiritual barrenness and how it affects ministry. As we study, God will reveal to us the causes of barrenness in our lives, churches and ministries.

It is important to diagnose barrenness when it exists in the ministry. The diagnosis of a problem often leads to the solution. Even in medicine, eighty per cent of our problems are solved when the right diagnosis is made. Many ministries are operating under a spirit of barrenness. Many pastors are unaware that they can have a greater level of fruitfulness. In this chapter, I will show you some signs you must look out for in order to detect barrenness in the ministry. If Jesus were standing by you, He would say these words to you:

> **Herein is my Father glorified, that ye bear much fruit; so shall ye be my disciples.**
>
> **John 15:8**

How to Diagnose Barrenness in Your Ministry

One way to diagnose barrenness is to understand how the dictionary defines it. If you apply these definitions to your church, you will know whether you are barren or not. God will show you if a spirit of barrenness is in operation. Let us now look at the dictionary definitions of barrenness and see how they apply to ministry.

1. Barrenness in the church means you are unfruitful.

2. Barrenness in the ministry means you are sterile.

3. Barrenness in the ministry means you are childless, heirless and issueless.

4. Barrenness in the ministry means you are non-productive.

5. Barrenness in the ministry means you are deficient in the production of souls, converts and disciples.

6. Barrenness in the ministry means you are not conceiving at all or producing at all.

7. Barrenness in the ministry means you are producing fruit in very small quantities.

8. Barrenness in the ministry means you are a wasteland.

9. Barrenness in the ministry means you are not producing normal fruit.

10. Barrenness in the ministry means you are bleak, abandoned and dry.

11. Barrenness in the ministry means you are depleted.

12. Barrenness in the ministry means you are not copious in producing fruits.

13. Barrenness in the ministry means you have a scanty attendance.

14. Barrenness in the ministry means you are dull and dry.

15. A barren individual does not produce after his kind.

Let us now look at the symptoms of barrenness within the church context. Examine your church and see whether barrenness exists.

How to Diagnose Barrenness in Your Church

Barrenness can be said to exist in a church if any of the following exists:

1. If there is no growth in the number of your church members.

2. If there are no converts, or no growth in the number of converts.

3. If there is no growth in church attendance.

4. If there is no growth in the number of full-time staff.

5. If there is no baptism, or no growth in the number of people baptized.

6. If there is the absence of healings and miracles.

7. If there is no growth in the number of leaders in the church.

8. If there is no increase in the knowledge of God.

9. If there is no growth in the depth of relationships.

10. If you have no visions and dreams given by the Holy Spirit or if there is no growth in the number of visions and dreams you receive from the Holy Spirit.

11. If there is no programme to send out missionaries or, no increase in the number of missionaries sent out.

12. If there is no growth in the finances of the church.

13. If there is no increase in the number of Scriptures you know.

14. If there is no growth in your experience in the ministry.

15. If there is the absence of, or no growth in the outreaches of the church.

16. If there is no growth in the length and depth of your prayer or no prayer at all.

17. If there is no increase in challenges and mountains to overcome.

18. If there is no challenge and inspiration to a greater vision.

19. If there is no growth in understanding.

20. If there is no growth in fellowships and branches in your ministry.

By the time you finish reading this book, all traces of barrenness will be gone from your life. Receive grace and wisdom to break out from the spirit of barrenness!

CHAPTER 2

Spiritual Blindness and Barrenness

For if these things be in you, and abound, they make you that YE SHALL NEITHER BE BARREN NOR UNFRUITFUL in the knowledge of our Lord Jesus Christ. BUT HE THAT LACKETH THESE THINGS IS BLIND, and cannot see afar off, and hath forgotten that he was purged from his old sins.

2 Peter 1:8-9

S piritual blindness is a major cause of barrenness. Why is that? Spiritually blind people cannot see heaven and hell and therefore they are not motivated to do anything for eternity. In their blindness, they see nothing, even though heaven and hell are real. Many people who stand in a pulpit are spiritually blind and that is why they do not talk anymore about heaven and hell. The rich man went to hell and Lazarus went to Abraham's bosom (Luke 16:19-26). These places are real, whether you believe in them or not. Anyone who does not talk about heaven and hell is spiritually blind. Spiritually blind people are completely oblivious of many realities. They cannot see eternity and they cannot also see their own state.

Spiritual blindness is the most dangerous spiritual condition that affects religious people. This is why many religious people are barren in the ministry. People who have been servants of God for some time are often affected by spiritual blindness. Most religious people in Jesus' time were spiritually blind. Jesus referred to them as blind ministers. In the twenty-third chapter of Matthew, Jesus described the Pharisees as being blind.

> Woe unto you, YE BLIND GUIDES, which say, whosoever shall swear by the temple, it is nothing; but whosoever shall swear by the gold of the temple, he is a debtor! YE FOOLS AND BLIND: for whether is greater, the gold, or the temple that sanctifieth the gold?
>
> Matthew 23:16-17

> YE FOOLS AND BLIND: for whether is greater, the gift, or the altar that sanctifieth the gift?
>
> Matthew 23:19

> YE BLIND GUIDES, which strain at a gnat, and swallow a camel ... Thou blind Pharisee, cleanse first that which is within the cup and platter, that the outside of them may be clean also.
>
> Matthew 23:24, 26

Once you have been a Christian for a long time, you are a candidate for spiritual blindness. Because this is such a serious condition, it is important to be able to define it and identify it when it is developing. Just as spiritual blindness enveloped the Pharisees, spiritual blindness envelopes long-standing Christians, ministers and churches. Let us look at how spiritual blindness developed in a Pharisee.

Four Signs of Spiritual Blindness

And he spake this parable unto certain which trusted in themselves that they were righteous, and despised others: Two men went up into the temple to pray; the one a Pharisee, and the other a publican. The Pharisee stood and prayed thus with himself, God, I thank thee, that I am not as other men are, extortioners, unjust, adulterers, or even as this publican. I fast twice in the week, I give tithes of all that I possess. And the publican, standing afar off, would not lift up so much as his eyes unto heaven, but smote upon his breast, saying, God be merciful to me a sinner. I tell you, this man went down to his house justified rather than the other: for every one that exalteth himself shall be abased; and he that humbleth himself shall be exalted.

Luke 18:9-14

This Pharisee was completely blind to the fact that he was far from God and not pleasing to God. He thought he was something that he was not. He was completely unaware of his true state. Spiritual blindness is something that affects the modern church. Notice how the Laodicean church was struck with a state of blindness.

(I know thy works, that thou art neither cold nor hot: I would thou wert cold or hot. So then because thou art lukewarm, and neither cold nor hot, I will spue thee out of my mouth. Because thou sayest, I am rich, and increased with goods, and have need of nothing; and KNOWEST NOT THAT THOU ART

WRETCHED, AND MISERABLE, AND POOR, AND BLIND,
AND NAKED: Revelation 3:15-17)

This blindness is a very serious condition because it caused
the Israelites to miss their Messiah when He came.

1.   Spiritually blind people are self-centred.

**Look not every man on his own things, but every man
also on the things of others.**

Philippians 2:4

Barrenness is caused by self-centredness. The spiritually
blind Pharisee in Luke 18:9-14 prayed "thus with himself." The
Pharisee was into himself. His life centred on himself and what
was important to him. There was nothing like "others." He never
thought of other people. Not thinking of other people makes you
barren, fruitless and useless.

Spiritually blind people are self-centred. Self-centredness has
two branches. On one hand, you are concerned with yourself and
you never think of helping or saving other people. The other
branch of self-centredness has to do with the fact that you do
not know what is happening in other people's ministries. You
think that everything great and important is happening in *your*
ministry. Many rich western ministries became spiritually blind
and they could not see what God was doing in poorer developing
countries. Often, rich and successful ministries are struck with
severe blindness until they become poor and unsuccessful
themselves. Then, suddenly, their eyes open and they find out
that there are other important parts of the body of Christ. They
find out that even though a church does not have a hundred and
fifty thousand dollars to give as honorarium it is still a valid
ministry.

2.   Spiritually blind people compare themselves with others:

**For we dare not make ourselves of the number, or
compare ourselves with some that commend themselves:**

but they measuring themselves by themselves, and comparing themselves among themselves, are not wise.

2 Corinthians 10:12

God intends for you to compare yourself with the standards of the word of God. Those who compare themselves with themselves are spiritually blind and barren. The spiritually blind Pharisee compared himself with the other person who was praying in the temple. Instead of concentrating on God and praying for his deficiencies, he was busy comparing himself with his fellow man. Comparing yourself with other people is a dangerous practice. No two things are really the same. There are reasons why things are the way they are.

3.   **Spiritually blind people despise others.**

Be of the same mind one toward another. Mind not high things, but condescend to men of low estate. Be not wise in your own conceits.

Romans 12:16

Failing to condescend to men of low estate will prevent you from becoming fruitful. Fruitfulness is caused by humble people who labour and work with the humble masses. Proud ministries despise small struggling ministries, seeing them as unanointed and irrelevant in the grand scheme of God's master plan. Spiritual blindness is a very serious condition that caused the Pharisees to miss Jesus Christ when He appeared.

4.   **Spiritually blind people have a deep sense of self-righteousness based on a set of rules that gives them confidence in their righteousness.**

For they being ignorant of God's righteousness, and GOING ABOUT TO ESTABLISH THEIR OWN RIGHTEOUSNESS, have not submitted themselves unto the righteousness of God.

Romans 10:3

Self-righteous people are often fruitless. Self-righteous people are full of idealism. They know what is right and they know what is wrong. But they are not fruitful. There was a time that listening to the radio was considered a sin by self-righteous people. There was a time that watching television was considered a sin by self-righteous people. There was a time that taking medicine was considered a sin by self-righteous people. There was a time that wearing trousers was thought to be a sin. All these rules were made at different times for different reasons.

Unfortunately, the numerous rules that spiritually blind people have, gives them a false sense of confidence. Paul said, they go about to establish their own righteousness and have not submitted themselves to the righteousness of God (Romans 10:3). Almost every Christian has a set of things that minister to him a sense of righteousness. When we do these things we feel righteous and we feel holy.

Spiritually blind people have a deep sense of self-righteousness based on a number of things that they have not been involved in. The fact that you have not done certain things before does not make you righteous.

Spiritually blind people have a set of things that they do not do, that give them even more confidence in their false righteousness. They say things like, "I have never committed this sin before. I have never smoked, I have never drank alcohol, I have never committed adultery, I have never failed to pay my tithes, I have never taken drugs."

They do not realise that they have not done these things because of God's mercy and grace. Beware of developing confidence in a list of things you have done or have not done. It will only lead to your spiritual blindness and barrenness.

CHAPTER 3

Short-sightedness and Barrenness

For if these things be in you, and abound, they make you THAT YE SHALL NEITHER BE BARREN NOR UNFRUITFUL in the knowledge of our Lord Jesus Christ. But he that lacketh these things is blind, and CANNOT SEE AFAR OFF, and hath forgotten that he was purged from his old sins.

2 Peter 1:8-9

S hort-sightedness is one of the crippling causes of barrenness. What is short-sightedness? Short-sightedness is when you cannot see far. Short-sightedness makes people do less and less for God.

What makes people settle into this state of barrenness? Why are many ministers of the gospel so barren?

Many ministers cannot see far. They see only a short distance from where they live but there is more to the world than the town where you live. There are millions of souls waiting in the corners of the earth.

Perhaps, you see only your one little church! Indeed, many people only see the community in which they live. They cannot see the next community. They do not know what is happening there and they do not care!

Many people see only their city. Indeed, many people only see a section of their city. Many people see only their tribe! Many people see only those who speak their language! Many people see only people from their country! Many people see only people in neighbouring countries! Many people see only people of their colour! Many Americans see only Americans! Many Nigerians see only Nigerians! Many Brazilians see only Brazilians!

What did Jesus teach us to see? He taught us to see as far as the end of the world. If your eye were seeing as far as Jesus taught us to see, you would not be as barren as you are. You would rise up knowing you had many things to do. If your eyes were open and you could see as far as God has asked you to see, you would see many nations, many tongues and many types of people, all waiting and hoping for the good news.

Barrenness has fallen on the church because it has become a short-sighted church where black people only see black people, Americans see only America and Africans see only Africa. It is time to open your eyes and see beyond!

Have you thought about how many ministers have a really international ministry? How many ministers have a really transnational ministry? Most pastors do not look very far! Because most ministers only look within their city, they have a small and limited ministry. It is time for you to break out of this barrenness by seeing afar.

CHAPTER 4

Forgetfulness and Barrenness

For if these things be in you, and abound, they make you that YE SHALL NEITHER BE BARREN NOR UNFRUITFUL in the knowledge of our Lord Jesus Christ. But he that lacketh these things is blind, and cannot see afar off, and HATH FORGOTTEN THAT HE WAS PURGED FROM HIS OLD SINS.

2 Peter 1:8-9

From the scripture above, we see that barrenness is also caused by forgetfulness. Forgetting, that salvation comes to people when they are purged from their old sins, by the blood of Jesus, is a major cause of barrenness.

Today, salvation is not a popular topic in the body of Christ. There are ministers who look down on the salvation message that Billy Graham preached. These people forget that salvation is the doorway through which sinners come into the body of Christ. Most ministers of the gospel cannot preach for one hour on the topic of salvation.

Salvation comes through the preaching of the gospel. We are not ashamed of the gospel of Jesus Christ. Why are we not ashamed of the gospel of Jesus Christ? Because the gospel of Jesus Christ has the power of salvation! When the gospel is preached, people are saved, people are born again and people are changed. That is why it is important to preach the gospel. We cannot be ashamed of the gospel. We cannot forget the gospel of Jesus Christ. That is how we found salvation.

For I am not ashamed of the gospel of Christ: for it is the power of God unto salvation to every one that believeth; to the Jew first, and also to the Greek.

Romans 1:16

The gospel of Jesus Christ is the news that God sent His Son into the world and His Son shed His blood that we might be saved. The gospel of Jesus Christ is the news about the cross and the great price that was paid for the salvation of the world. The gospel of Jesus Christ is a specific message that cannot be altered or changed whatsoever.

Paul told the Corinthians that he was determined not to know anything except Jesus Christ and Him crucified. He did not want to have any business dealings with the Corinthians. He did not want discussions on investment opportunities. Paul did not want to set up a university in Corinth. Paul did not want to build a hospital in Corinth. Paul did not want to build a school. Paul did

18

not want to improve the education in Corinth. Paul did not want to meet the government leaders. Paul wanted to discuss Jesus Christ with the Corinthians. His message had to do with the crucifixion of Christ and what it meant.

> And I, brethren, when I came to you, came not with excellency of speech or of wisdom, declaring unto you the testimony of God. For I determined not to know any thing among you, save Jesus Christ, and him crucified.
>
> 1 Corinthians 2:1-2

Apostle Paul was determined to stick with the gospel that he had received. He did not want to deviate from the core message of Jesus Christ and the salvation that He had brought us. Notice his remarks to the Corinthians. Please read the details of the gospel message below.

Moreover, brethren, I declare unto you the gospel which I preached unto you, which also ye have received, and wherein ye stand; By which also ye are saved, if ye keep in memory what I preached unto you, unless ye have believed in vain.

> For I delivered unto you first of all that which I also received, how that Christ died for our sins according to the scriptures; And that he was buried, and that he rose again the third day according to the scriptures:
>
> 1 Corinthians 15:1-4

Today, many top leaders in the church have forgotten the gospel of Jesus Christ. Perhaps they are even ashamed of this message. One pastor said a religion that speaks about the blood is not attractive. Another person said, "If we want to attract people, we cannot emphasize on such gory subjects as the cross, the crucifixion and the blood of Jesus." Another pastor declared that preaching about the prosperity and the good life that Jesus offers is more important than preaching about the cross, the blood and the suffering of Jesus Christ.

Indeed, from the topics that people preach about today in many churches, we can see that prosperity, a good life, a successful life, a happy life, a good family, nice children, good investments and many others are more important than preaching the gospel of Jesus Christ. Indeed, these are the things that are emphasized in the church today.

But it is a big mistake to set aside the cross, the blood, the crucifixion and the suffering of Jesus Christ and replace it with teachings on prosperity, a good life, a successful life, a happy life, a good family, nice children, good investments and good houses. It is a mistake to teach people to be millionaires instead of teaching them about Jesus Christ. Do not be impressed by backslidden pastors who preach as though they are lecturers in a secular university. Do not be impressed by smooth words and nice rhyming sayings. Smooth words are not necessarily good words.

> The words of his mouth were smoother than butter, but war was in his heart: his words were softer than oil, yet were they drawn swords.
>
> Psalm 55:21

Barrenness has fallen on the church because we have forgotten that salvation comes through the preaching of the gospel of Jesus Christ.

I once interacted with a pastor who mostly preaches and writes about how to make money. I asked him what he was taught when he became a Christian. He mentioned many well-known Christian topics like discipleship, sacrifice and salvation. Then I asked him why he was always preaching about money. I wondered why he would not want to teach Christians what he was taught that established him in Christ.

It is sad that people have forgotten how they became Christians! It is sad that people have forgotten how salvation happens in the first place! Indeed, forgetting is the principal cause of barrenness.

CHAPTER 5

Aqar Barrenness of Your Ministry

There shall nothing cast their young, nor be barren (*Aqar*), in thy land: the number of thy days I will fulfil.

Exodus 23:26

Several Hebrew words are translated into the word "barren" or "barrenness." Each of these words has a special meaning and throws the light of revelation on the subject of barrenness.

AQAR

This word means "the destruction or removal of generative organs". It also means "to have non-functioning organs", "to be barren or sterile". It is used in reference to people like Sarah, Rachel, Hannah, the mother of Samson, and Rebecca.

But Sarai was barren; she had no child.

Genesis 11:30

And there was a certain man of Zorah, of the family of the Danites, whose name was Manoah; and his wife was barren, and bare not. And the angel of the LORD appeared unto the woman, and said unto her, Behold now, thou art barren, and bearest not: but thou shalt conceive, and bear a son.

Judges 13:2-3

And Isaac intreated the LORD for his wife, because she was barren: and the LORD was intreated of him, and Rebekah his wife conceived.

Genesis 25:21

They that were full have hired out themselves for bread; and they that were hungry ceased: so that the barren hath born seven; and she that hath many children is waxed feeble.

1 Samuel 2:5

Thou shalt be blessed above all people: there shall not be male or female barren among you, or among your cattle.

Deuteronomy 7:14

There shall nothing cast their young, nor be barren (AQAR), in thy land: the number of thy days I will fulfil.

Exodus 23:26

Ministers suffering from *AQAR* barrenness are deficient in the generative aspect of ministry. This means they are deficient in the *outreach* and *fruit-bearing* aspects of ministry. They are unable to give birth to anything in the ministry. Such pastors may have many activities but these programmes do not bring much fruit for the ministry.

One way of fighting barrenness is to consider the outreach aspect of your ministry. Do you have crusades? Do you plant new churches? The absence of crusades, breakfast meetings, witnessing campaigns and real ministry work, shows a deficiency in the generative aspect of your ministry.

Barren people who are members of the church receive the Word and probably have the messages. They may even be involved in other activities of the church. They are seen at prayer meetings and become "fat" spiritually. However, such people will not be involved in ministry, evangelism or soul winning. This proves that they have a deficiency in their spiritual generative organs.

CHAPTER 6

Shakol Barrenness of Ministry

I will also send wild beasts among you, which shall rob you of your children, and destroy your cattle, and make you few in number; and your high ways shall be desolate. (SHAKOL).

Leviticus 26:22

S everal Hebrew words are translated into the word "barren" or "barrenness." Each of these words has a special meaning and throws the light of revelation on the subject of barrenness.

SHAKOL

This means "to miscarry, to suffer abortion, to be bereaved of children, to be barren, to cast your young, to make childless and to be deprived of children".

And the men of the city said unto Elisha, Behold, I pray thee, the situation of this city is pleasant, as my lord seeth: but the water is naught, and the ground barren.

2 Kings 2:19

I will also send wild beasts among you, which shall rob you of your children, and destroy your cattle, and make you few in number; and your high ways shall be desolate. (SHAKOL)

Leviticus 26:22

Any minister experiencing *SHAKOL* cannot keep the souls that God gives him. Such ministers constantly cast their young and suffer abortions. They cannot sustain growth and are unable to continue in the things that God gives to them. Many churches receive large numbers of visitors and, even, converts. You must work on keeping these converts. You must make sure that your visitors come again.

I always pray over my members. I pray to God, "Lord, when they go, let them come back to church. As they come back, let them come with more people." I pray that each member becomes a minister and that each minister gives birth to a church. This kind of prayer counteracts *shakol* barrenness.

Another reason why some other churches are unable to break out is that they attack their young leaders. They kill fresh blood. The leaders do not allow mavericks to flourish around them. The anointing on all of us is greater than the anointing on one person. You must allow fresh leaders and pastors to be released under your ministry. The fastest growth always occurs when there are multiple ministers working together.

CHAPTER 7

Melechah Barrenness of Ministry

And the men of the city said unto Elisha, Behold, I pray thee, the situation of this city is pleasant, as my lord seeth: but the water is naught, and the ground barren (*MELECHAH*). And he said, Bring me a new cruse, and put salt therein. And they brought it to him. And he went forth unto the spring of the waters, and cast the salt in there, and said, Thus saith the LORD, I have healed these waters; there shall not be from thence any more death or barren land. So the waters were healed unto this day, according to the saying of Elisha which he spake.

2 Kings 2:19-22

S everal Hebrew words are translated into the word "barren" or "barrenness." Each of these words has a special meaning and throws more light on the subject of barrenness.

MELECHAH

This word means "a salted land, a desert or a barren land". It speaks of no produce and no life. The land is dead to any kind of seed. People suffering from *MELECHAH* are like spiritually salted lands. In spite of what you pour into them, they are unable to bear fruit. They are incapable of germinating seeds.

A cursory glance at every congregation will reveal several "salted lands" staring at you. Mercy and atonement! They have been in the church for many years and have heard many sermons. They have been anointed and prayed for specially, but they still cannot bear fruit. Much is poured into them but little can be expected from these salted ones.

For he shall be like the heath in the desert, and shall not see when good cometh; but shall inhabit the parched places in the wilderness, in a salt land and not inhabited.

Jeremiah 17:6

There are also salted churches. No matter the input, the church does not grow. No new churches are planted from that church. Until the salted land is healed, there will be no fruit.

He turneth rivers into a wilderness, and the watersprings into dry ground; A fruitful land into barrenness, for the wickedness of them that dwell therein.

Psalm 107:33-34

And the men of the city said unto Elisha, Behold, I pray thee, the situation of this city is pleasant, as my Lord seeth: but the water is naught, and the ground barren (MELECHAH). And he said, Bring me a new cruse, and put salt therein. And they brought it to him. And

he went forth unto the spring of the waters, and cast the salt in there, and said, Thus saith the LORD, I have healed these waters; there shall not be from thence any more death or barren land. So the waters were healed unto this day, according to the saying of Elisha which he spake.

2 Kings 2:19-22

A pastor who is a salted land does not give rise to other pastors of his own kind. He remains in the church he pastors, but cannot bring forth other pastors. Break out of the salted state and start to think of birthing more pastors and more churches!

I remember the story of a church that could not grow. No matter what happened and no matter who preached, there was no breakthrough. One day, a visiting pastor was waiting on the Lord and he had a vision. Way up in the ceiling he saw a demon sitting above the congregation. This evil spirit had greatly affected the church for many years. God opened the pastor's eyes to see the "salt" that was making the church barren. He dealt with the evil spirit and commanded it to leave.

After that experience, the church began to grow in leaps and bounds. I believe there are real "salted land" situations that need the healing hand of God. I see God removing the saltiness from your life, church and ministry!

CHAPTER 8

Otser Barrenness of Ministry

The grave; and the barren (*OTSER*) womb; the earth that is not filled with water; and the fire that saith not, It is enough.

Proverbs 30:16

Hebrew words are important in understanding the revelation God is trying to bring to us. One of these words is the word "*Otser*."

OTSER

This Hebrew word means "To inclose, to hold back and to maintain". It also means "To close up, to restrain, and retain". In addition, it means "To shut up, to withhold and to stop".

The grave; and the barren (*OTSER*) womb; the earth that is not filled with water; and the fire that saith not, It is enough.

Proverbs 30:16

People suffering from this kind of barrenness hold back intentionally. They know a lot, but they hold back and refuse to be fruitful. Pastors with *OTSER* barrenness have the finances and the anointing to break forth in ministry. However, they give their strength to other things like orphanages, schools and social work. Some of them are more concerned about being politically influential and socially acceptable than doing the work of God. The drive for ministry is restrained!

Such people can do many things for the Lord but are restrained. They hold back their talents even though they are usually experienced people who could do much more for Jesus. It is often because they have decided to give their strength and talents to other things.

If you are a pastor, you will notice in your congregation people who are leaders of Old Boys' Associations or even political groups. They have time for politics, soccer, MBA, or PhD courses, and other activities. However, when it comes to the work of God, they are enclosed and restrained. They are reserved when it comes to prayer and worship, but vocal when it comes to discussing politics and other issues. These are the people suffering from *otser*.

CHAPTER 9

Tsiyah Barrenness of Ministry

I will open rivers in high places, and fountains in the midst of the valleys: I will make the wilderness a pool of water, and the dry LAND (*TSIYAH*) springs of water.

Isaiah 41:18

ebrew words are important in understanding the revelation God is trying to bring to us. One of these words is the word "*Tsiyah.*" God is setting you free from this type of barrenness.

TSIYAH

This word speaks of being "Parched and barren". It speaks of "A drought, a dry land and a wilderness".

O God, thou art my God; early will I seek thee: my soul thirsteth for thee, my flesh longeth for thee in a dry and thirsty land, where no water is;

Psalm 63:1

I will open rivers in high places, and fountains in the midst of the valleys: I will make the wilderness a pool of water, and the dry LAND (*TSIYAH*) springs of water.

Isaiah 41:18

A church suffering from *TSIYAH* is often dry of the Spirit. It is a wilderness devoid of worship, prayer and the lifting up of hands. That kind of church is usually very secular and logical in its approach to life and the ministry. Spiritual dryness and the lack of worship is a true sign of barrenness. Introducing new worship songs will often fight against this kind of barrenness.

Sometimes, changing your worship leader will lead to a major change in your church. Changing your choir leader and the type of songs your choir sings can also greatly affect your church. Perhaps if the choir were to sing songs about soul winning and reaching the lost, many outreach ministries would begin.

Do not wait forever to make the changes you need in order to bring fruitfulness to your ministry.

CHAPTER 10

Steiras Barrenness of Ministry

And they had no child, because that Elisabeth was barren (*steiras*), and they both were now well stricken in years.

Luke 1:7

There are also Greek words that are translated *barren* or *barrenness*. These words also help to throw more light on the subject of spiritual and ministerial barrenness. Through your understanding of these words you will overcome every type of barrenness in your life.

STEIRAS

And they had no child, because that Elisabeth was barren (*steiras*), and they both were now well stricken in years... And, behold, thy cousin Elisabeth, she hath also conceived a son in her old age: and this is the sixth month with her, who was called barren.

Luke 1:7, 36

For it is written, Rejoice, thou barren that bearest not; break forth and cry, thou that travailest not: for the desolate hath many more children than she which hath an husband.

Galatians 4:27

This word means, "To be stiff and unnatural". It speaks of sterility and barrenness. *Stiffness* describes people who are unyielding and disobedient to the Word of God.

Anyone who is disobedient to the Word will be barren. Such people love to look distinguished and diplomatic. Sometimes they pretend to be spiritual but in reality they are not.

Churches often have these unspiritual and stiff people sitting in the front row. This can prevent growth and induce the *STEIRAS* atmosphere, which promotes barrenness. You will notice that growing churches are full of lively, exuberant and excited people dancing and praising the Lord.

The church is not a who-is-who parade! It is time to remove the "deep freezers" from the prominent positions we have given them.

CHAPTER 11

Argos Barrenness of Your Ministry

For if these things be in you, and abound, they make you that ye shall neither be barren nor unfruitful (*ARGOS*) in the knowledge of our Lord Jesus Christ.

2 Peter 1:8

G reek words are important in understanding the revelation God is trying to bring to us. One of these words is the word "*Argos*."

ARGOS

This word means, "Inactive, unemployed, lazy and useless". It also speaks of "Being idle, slow and barren". Laziness is one of the principal causes of unfruitfulness in ministry. Lazy people are inactive in church. Their laziness makes them useless to God.

For if these things be in you, and abound, they make you that ye shall neither be barren nor unfruitful (*ARGOS*) in the knowledge of our Lord Jesus Christ.

2 Peter 1:8

Unfortunately, the church is made up of masses of spiritually inactive people.   To break this type of barrenness, it is important to preach about diligence. It is important to teach the congregation that they must win souls for the Lord.

CHAPTER 12

The Barrenness of Old Age

But Sarai was barren; she had no child.

Genesis 11:30

Now Sarai Abram's wife bare him no children: and she had an handmaid, an Egyptian, whose name was Hagar. And Sarai said unto Abram, Behold now, the LORD hath restrained me from bearing: I pray thee, go in unto my maid; it may be that I may obtain children by her. And Abram hearkened to the voice of Sarai. And Sarai Abram's wife took Hagar her maid the Egyptian, after Abram had dwelt ten years in the land of Canaan, and gave her to her husband Abram to be his wife. And he went in unto Hagar, and she conceived: and when she saw that she had conceived, her mistress was despised in her eyes.

Genesis 16:1-4

We all know the story of Abraham and Sarah. You could consider Sarah as a type of church. You could also consider her as a type of minister. Sarah could be likened to a pastor who is not bearing as much fruit because he is old. Many older churches are now barren. Perhaps they started out as fruitful ministries but as the years have gone by, the anointing and the river of the Holy Spirit is replaced by tradition, rituals and custom. Sarah could be likened to a kind of church in which there is no longer life because of old age.

You can fight old age barrenness by doing these things:

1. Do not transfer the duty of outreach and ministry to anyone else.

According to Genesis 16:1-2, Sarah shifted the responsibility of child-bearing to someone else. In an attempt to bear fruit, Sarah shifted her work to Hagar. This was a man-made effort to overcome barrenness. She tried to overcome barrenness in the wrong way. Do not try to delegate what you must do yourself. Pastors must rise up and become fruitful themselves. Pastors must pray themselves and preach the Word.

2. Do not reject the prophetic word.

Therefore Sarah laughed within herself, saying, After I am waxed old shall I have pleasure, my Lord being old also?

Genesis 18:12

Sarah laughed when she heard the prophecy about Isaac. Receive the visitation of God for your life through revelations, dreams and the spoken Word. Older people tend to mock at the prophetic word, seeing it as impossible. They are experienced in life and much more cynical and scornful about prophetic direction.

> *...Believe in the Lord your God, and you shall be established; believe His prophets and you shall prosper.*
>
> **2 Chronicles 20:20 (NKJV)**

Prophetic messages can make a difference in your ministry. Years ago, I received a message from a prophet. He saw me carrying a flaming torch and leading many people. He gave this message to me in 1980. Forty-two years have gone by and this prophecy remains in my heart as a true vision. It encouraged me to do the work of God as a student. It encouraged me to persist in the ministry even after school.

3. **Believe in God, His prophets and in the preaching of His Word.**

> **And God said unto Abraham, as for Sarai thy wife, thou shalt not call her name Sarai, but Sarah shall her name be.**
>
> **Genesis 17:15**

Walk in your calling. You must overcome the greatest enemies of the faith walk: fear and intimidation. Walking in fear and intimidation will not lead to fruitfulness in ministry.

4. **Take the practical step that leads to fruitfulness even if it looks like something for younger people.**

> **For Sarah conceived, and bare Abraham a son in his old age...And Abraham called the name of his son... Isaac.**
>
> **Genesis 21:2-3**

Isaac was not supernaturally conceived as was the case of Christ Jesus. He was conceived by the normal method of sexual intercourse. Sarah had to undress and act like an energetic young lady with a youthful husband! Abraham and Sarah were forced to engage in sexual happiness in their nineties. Can you imagine a ninety-year-old, menopausal woman acting like a pretty youthful bride again?

Decide to be youthful, zealous, emotional, exciting, energetic and adventurous again. This will break the spell and curse of barrenness over your ministry. Sarah had sex with her husband at the age of ninety. No matter what prophecy is spoken over your life, there will always be some practical steps you have to take.

Some ministers are too "old" in their actions and thoughts! Some amount of youthfulness is needed in the ministry. Youthfulness is necessary for fruitfulness!

CHAPTER 13

The Barrenness of Familiarity

David went home so he could ask the Lord to bless his family. But Saul's daughter Michal went out and started yelling at him. 'You were really great today!' she said. "You acted like a dirty old man, dancing half-naked in front of your servants' slave girls." David told her, "The Lord didn't choose your father or anyone else in your family to be the leader of His people. The Lord chose me and I was celebrating in honour of him. I'll show you how great I can be! I'll even be disgusted to myself. But those slave girls you talked about will still honour me!" Michal never had any children.

2 Samuel 6:20-23 (Contemporary English Version)

Familiarity is a major cause of unfruitfulness and barrenness. Familiar people cannot be fruitful.

Familiarity is the greatest block to the anointing. It cuts off the flow of the anointing that is needed for ministry and church growth. Ministry is a spiritual thing and unless spiritual principles are obeyed, the ministry dries up and barrenness results.

Michal is a type of barren ministry. She suffered from familiarity towards her husband. She paid for it by becoming barren. Many people have become barren in ministry because they became too familiar with the man of God.

David went home so he could ask the Lord to bless his family. But Saul's daughter Michal went out and started yelling at him. 'You were really great today!' she said. "You acted like a dirty old man, dancing half-naked in front of your servants' slave girls." David told her, "The Lord didn't choose your father or anyone else in your family to be the leader of His people. The Lord chose me and I was celebrating in honour of him. I'll show you how great I can be! I'll even be disgusted to myself. But those slave girls you talked about will still honour me!" Michal never had any children.

2 Samuel 6:20-23 (Contemporary English Version)

Familiarity means "To know someone or something so well and in such a way as to cause you to lose your admiration, respect and sense of awe".

It also connotes a sense of becoming presumptuous where a person is too confident in a way that shows a lack of respect.

1.   **Familiarity was the cause of Michal's barrenness.**

2.   **Familiarity is still the cause of spiritual barrenness in many Christians today.**

3.   Familiarity is the greatest block to receiving God's power from God's men.

4.   No matter how great the gift of God, it is neutralized by familiarity.

Jesus was the greatest healer and teacher, yet His anointing was neutralized by the presence of familiar people.

And he went out from thence, and came into his own country; and his disciples follow him. And when the sabbath day was come, he began to teach in the synagogue: and many hearing him were astonished, saying, From whence hath this man these things? and what wisdom is this which is given unto him, that even such mighty works are wrought by his hands? Is not this the carpenter, the son of Mary ... And they were offended at him. And he could there do no mighty work, save that he laid his hands upon a few sick folk, and healed them.

Mark 6:1-3,5

This Scripture shows us that Jesus could not perform miracles in His hometown. They knew Him too well to receive Him as the Son of God. They had questions about His parents, His family and His background.

Moses who commanded a pillar of fire by night and a pillar of cloud by day, could not impress his own sister Miriam. She criticized him about his marriage and suffered for it. My heart is often closed to those who are familiar towards me. I simply do not flow towards them. I can virtually sense the questions in the hearts of people suffering from familiarity towards me.

Familiarity drives men of God away from their colleagues, friends and family. It leads them towards the non-familiar, the poor, the forgotten and neglected ones. This is where the outsiders come in. Outsiders often come in to replace people who have become too familiar with the anointed one.

Those Who have the Barrenness of Familiarity

There are certain groups of people who easily become prey to familiarity. These are usually people who know the man of God closely.

1. **Being a colleague or friend of the man of God can make you familiar and barren.**

These people also experience familiarity. They have been around you for so long and seen your vicissitudes. It is easy to slip and slide into familiarity. Sometimes it would be better not to know someone closely in order not to develop an air of familiarity.

When I started my church as a medical student, very few of my colleagues were able to receive from me. They knew me too well and would say in their hearts, "Is this not Dag? We know him and we know his class. We saw him struggling at an exam last week. We know when he passes and when he fails! How can this lanky boy call himself a pastor?"

2. **Being a relative of a man of God can make you familiar and barren.**

Relatives also suffer from familiarity. They would say, "Is this not Azoyzoy's (my father's nickname) son? We carried him when he was a baby."

They ask, "Do you remember me? I carried you when you were two years old."

They say, "I knew your father very well."

With this background, how can such people receive me as a man of God?

3. **Being married to a man of God can make you familiar and barren.**

Pastors' wives often suffer from severe familiarity. Just like Michal, they are not impressed with their husbands when everyone is impressed.

They say things like, "I know you. No one knows you better than I do. I am the only one who can tell you certain things! I am not one of those people who give you praise and affirmation in the office! If people knew how you really were, they would be surprised. No one knows what you are really like."

In a sense, they are right about all these things, but the fact is that they have become victims of familiarity!

4.   Constantly choosing to sit at the back of the church is a sign of familiarity and barrenness.

Familiarity is when you are no longer intrigued and excited about the pastor and his preaching. You do not bother to come near anymore. Familiar people just sit at the back and observe from a distance.

Once, I attended a Kenneth Hagin conference in Tulsa, Oklahoma. When I entered the hall, the ushers tried to give me a seat at the back.

I thought to myself, "How can I sit at the back when Kenneth Hagin is preaching?" "I want to be as near as possible!" I negotiated with the usher and even made friends with him.

I told him, "Sir, you don't know where I have come from."

I continued, "I have flown thousands and thousands of miles to be here today. I need to be as near as possible. There is no way I can go upstairs or even to the back."

He seemed to understand and I eventually had my way. Unbelievably, I managed to sit on the second row. I was so excited when Kenneth Hagin walked by my seat as he preached.

You see, when you are familiar, seeing a man of God nearby or from afar makes no difference. Later on, I had a discussion with the principal of their Bible School. I asked him if they had any problems with their students. To my surprise he told me that they did. Their main problem was familiarity.

He said to me, "There are some students who do not come for important conferences like these."

He lamented, "This is a great prophet of God that people come to listen to from all over the world. But right here, there are students who do not bother to cross the road to come to church." You see, familiarity breeds contempt.

Familiarity is all about knowing someone so well that it causes you to lose your admiration and respect.

5.   Sleeping during preaching is a sign of familiarity and barrenness.

Yawning is often a sign of boredom. A familiar person is presumptuous and arrogantly assumes he knows what is coming. Often, people who yawn during the preaching of the Word are saying, "I know this sermon, I know what is coming. I know his line of thought. This man has nothing new to say."

Sleep comes when we are tired. But sometimes it comes because of monotony and boredom. When the man of God fails to intrigue you anymore, you may find yourself sleeping as he preaches. Familiarity breeds disloyalty. Familiarity created Judas. Judas is referred to as "*mine own familiar friend*" (Psalm 41:9). When people are familiar, they lose their respect and they cross boundaries they should never cross.

Familiarity makes people say things they should never say. Michal became a critic of the man after God's own heart. David had built a tabernacle but she was not impressed. God called David, "a man after mine own heart" (Acts 13:22) but she, a mere mortal, despised him. Imagine that God is impressed but you are not impressed. Is it not amazing!

Familiarity often stems from jealousy and carnality. Michal was jealous of the girls who seemed to appreciate David's ministry. She disliked the fact that David seemed to be impressed with these young whippersnappers.

> **…Michal the daughter of Saul came out to meet David, and said, HOW GLORIOUS WAS THE KING OF ISRAEL TO DAY, who uncovered himself today in the eyes of the handmaids of his servants, as one of the vain fellows shamelessly uncovereth himself!**
>
> **2 Samuel 6:20**

When Miriam criticized Moses, she no longer saw him as God's anointed. She moved into the flesh and became a disloyal rebel.

> **And Miriam and Aaron spake against Moses because of the Ethiopian woman whom he had married: for he had married an Ethiopian woman.**
>
> **Numbers 12:1**

Judas was the highest kind of traitor. He paid the ultimate price for allowing himself to be deceived by familiarity.

> **Yea, mine own familiar friend, in whom I trusted, which did eat of my bread, hath lifted up his heel against me.**
>
> **Psalm 41:9**

I have had different people getting close to me at different times in my life. Circumstances can sometimes cause people to associate closely with the man of God. Under such circumstances, the person is susceptible to the spirit of familiarity. It takes spiritual discipline not to become familiar.

I have noticed in my life and ministry how people become over-familiar when given the slightest chance. Let me just remind you of the definition of familiarity. *Familiarity* means "To know someone or something very well and in such a way as to cause you to lose your admiration, respect and sense of awe. It also connotes a sense of becoming presumptuous, where a person is too confident in a way that shows a lack of respect".

One day, a young lady was having a problem in her marriage. Her husband said to her, "I am going to report you to the Bishop."

She retorted, "I don't care. He also has problems."

I smiled when I heard this. I knew that it was only familiarity that was rearing its head. Perhaps, I was wrong to have allowed this person to spend a few nights in our home. On another occasion, another relative who had spent a few days with our family was having some problems. After counselling this relative, she seemed to have understood what I had shared with her. She thanked me and seemed genuinely blessed.

Unfortunately, she told someone later that I am a man of knowledge and not a man of experience. What she was saying was that I had no experience in the kind of problem she had and my advice was therefore theoretical!

I thought to myself, "I have now become a man of knowledge without experience. It is only because I had allowed this person to relate so closely to my family and I that she had the nerve to make such a comment."

Sometimes it is better to know someone from afar so that you can continue to receive from his ministry. When you are too familiar with your pastor, you can mistakenly see him as "a man of knowledge without experience"!

In your relationship with a man of God, are you becoming familiar? In the next chapter, I will describe some signs which will help you determine the extent to which you are familiar. Remember that familiarity is the best way to kill the anointing. It has the greatest capability of neutralizing the power of God's gift.

6. **Not listening to messages preached by the man of God is a sign of familiarity and barrenness.**

I have rarely seen a fruitful person who does not listen to messages. Someone who listens to preaching messages has not become over familiar with the pastor's voice. He sees it as an opportunity to be continuously blessed by the pastor when he is not around. Have you asked yourself why you do not listen to messages anymore? The answer may be familiarity.

7. Not reading the books of your man of God is a sign of familiarity and barrenness.

I notice how people come from afar to buy my books. There are times people have travelled many miles to acquire and "devour" large quantities of my books and preaching messages. Amazingly, my own church members often pass by these same books and messages and instead call for two meat pies and a bottle of Coca-Cola. Familiarity causes you to lose your sense of wonder and intrigue.

8. Discussing the background of the man of God is a sign of familiarity and barrenness.

Every man of God basically, is a "man". Since he is a man, he goes through what all men go through. No man that God ever chose has a perfect life. Everyone of them has a past! He has a family. He has failings. He has an imperfect marriage. He has challenges just like everyone else.

It is easy to pick on any aspect of his natural life and neutralize him. Discussing the man of God in a natural way is a sure sign that you have lost your sense of fascination for him. This is the surest way to cancel out the effect of the anointing on your man of God.

When Jesus preached in His hometown, the Scripture says in Luke 4:28, "...when they heard these things, they were filled with wrath." The familiar people were angry at Jesus' sermon. But when He preached in Galilee according to Luke 4:32 "They were astonished at His doctrine". The hometown people were simply amazed at Jesus' ministry.

Notice also that familiarity happened in Nazareth, Jesus' hometown. Meanwhile, they were awestruck in a city of Galilee about two hundred kilometres from Jesus' hometown of

Nazareth. The difference here is that in Nazareth, people knew His background; in Galilee, they did not.

9. **Discussing the family issues of the man of God is a sign of familiarity and barrenness.**

Is not this the carpenter, the son of Mary, the brother of James, and Joses, and of Juda, and Simon? and are not his sisters here with us? And they were offended at him.

Mark 6:3

By doing this, you are cutting yourself from receiving God's miracle for your life. When Jesus went to His hometown, there was a long discussion as to who He really was. Someone may have said, "I know that boy. He is my nephew. He and his father have repaired my wardrobes and cupboards for many years."

Jesus could do very few miracles because of the high level of familiarity and doubt in the city. Do not let familiarity cut off your blessing!

10. **Fault-finding and magnifying faults is a sign of familiarity and barrenness.**

Whenever you think of the great men of God you respect, you do not often think of their faults.

When there is a visiting preacher, no one considers whether he is impatient or easily angered. No one thinks of whether this man is in debt or whether he has an extravagant lifestyle. All we do is to receive the ministry of this man of God.

However, these are thoughts that occur to us about men of God we are familiar with. We think, "He must be angry today, this man is not patient." As he preaches we say to ourselves, "We understand what he is saying; why does he not progress to the next point?"

I remember years ago, I had a church member who really enjoyed my messages. She recommended me highly to many people who later joined the church. However, as time went by, she became familiar with my preaching and with me.

One day after church she said to me, "I think you went over last week's point for too long." She continued, "There was very little time for the new points that you brought up." A few weeks later, she made another remark, "The repetition in your preaching is too much." After this I noticed the frown on her face each time I preached. This lady eventually stopped coming to church.

She might have been right, but what she did not realize was that, I was preaching to people who came to church one week and missed the other week. I virtually had a new crowd every week. I may have had my faults, but God has worked through me in spite of them. Have you removed the log in your own eye? Why are you concentrating so hard on the speck in the pastor's eye? Familiarity has made you critical!

11. Evaluating and rating men of God is a sign of familiarity and barrenness.

Democracy in its essential nature, calls on us to evaluate our leaders constantly. This is what enables us to vote for the right person. Unfortunately, many are deceived when they think that this same practice of evaluation must be brought into the church.

I was driving home one day after church when one of the people in the car with me asked a question. He asked, "How did you find the sermon?"

The car was quiet for a moment then someone said, "I think he did well, I will give him 70%."

Then an older man said, "No, no, no. He deserves about 49%."

Someone asked, "Why 49%, the message wasn't too bad?"

I mused to myself, "This poor pastor is being assessed by his congregation members." His members had now become familiar!

12. Not believing the man of God's advice is a sign of familiarity and barrenness.

When you regard someone highly, you cherish whatever advice he has to offer. As familiarity sets in, it becomes more and more difficult to accept advice. Every time advice is given there is a reason not to follow it.

13. Having no regard for the anointing is a sign of familiarity and barrenness.

The fact that he is even anointed does not occur to you. All you see are natural things. If your eyes are on the natural, you will see weakness, dishonour and corruption.

So also is the resurrection of the dead. It is sown in CORRUPTION; it is raised in incorruption: It is sown in DISHONOUR; it is raised in glory: it is sown in WEAKNESS; it is raised in power:

1 Corinthians 15:42-43

14. Not honouring and appreciating your man of God is a sign of familiarity and barrenness.

As you get used to your pastor, it is easy to take him for granted. We often neglect those with whom we are familiar. I remember one pastor who had never been honoured by his congregation. However, his church was constantly blessing a particular honoured visiting preacher. When this visiting preacher came to hold a convention, the crowds would gather and the people would express their appreciation to the visiting minister. They would bring money and gifts to honour him. But the church would never honour its own pastor.

The deception here is that the visitor is the one who is sent from God to them. *But the reality is that their own familiar pastor is the one who labours over them with love.*

I teach my church members that it is biblical to honour and give gifts to a man of God. This is not to enhance the minister's lifestyle but it is to honour God's gift and to kill the spirit of familiarity.

CHAPTER 14

Mysterious Barrenness

But unto Hannah he gave a worthy portion; for he loved Hannah: but THE LORD HAD SHUT UP HER WOMB.

1 Samuel 1:5

Many people suffer from a mysterious form of barrenness. Barrenness is mysterious when the cause is unclear. What is the mysterious cause of my fruitlessness? What am I missing? Why is my church not growing? Why is my ministry not developing? Why is it that everything I start and do is not blooming and flourishing as I expect? There are many times you cannot easily find the cause of barrenness and unfruitfulness. In medical science, there are many cases of barrenness where the cause is uncertain. Indeed, sometimes doctors are happy to just find a reason for the barrenness. Hannah is a good example of a mysteriously barren ministry that became fruitful. She is one of the great examples of someone who broke out of the power of barrenness and became very fruitful.

The key to breaking out of mysterious barrenness is intercession prayers, where you go into the mysterious spirit realm and obtain the solution and an answer. When you speak in tongues you speak mysteries to God! Speaking in tongues causes you to address mysteries with mysteries. The great key that Hannah demonstrated was again the key of intercession. Great ministries are born out of intercession.

Hannah was a barren ministry. Hannah was in serious trouble. She desperately needed a breakthrough. She did not just *doodle and dawdle*. To doodle and dawdle means "To hang around, loiter, to waste time and to make wavy impressions". She was dead serious about what she wanted from God.

Dear pastor, fervent prayer will make you give birth to a new dimension in ministry. Intercession will always lead to new spiritual children.

Now Hannah, she spake in her heart; only her lips moved, but her voice was not heard: therefore Eli thought she had been drunken.

1 Samuel 1:13

The Church prayed fervently for the power of the Holy Spirit to be upon their leaders. That is how they broke through and became fruitful.

And being let go, they went to their own company, and reported all that the chief priests and elders had said unto them. And when they heard that, they lifted up their voice to God with one accord, and said, Lord, thou art God, which hast made heaven, and earth, and the sea, and all that in them is: ... By stretching forth thine hand to heal; and that signs and wonders may be done by the name of thy holy child Jesus. And when they had prayed, the place was shaken where they were assembled together; and they were all filled with the Holy Ghost, and they spake the word of God with boldness.

Acts 4:23-24, 30-31

God heard their prayer and look at the results.

When a church begins to pray fervently there are always results. The word of God is preached when prayer goes forth. Churches spring up when the word of God is preached.

It is important to stress that *fervent* prayer is what makes the difference. Sometimes, I look at people who claim to be having a prayer meeting. You see some of them sleeping and others just whiling away time. How would you feel if someone fell asleep while talking to you? You would think that he is either disrespectful or very uninterested in you.

Jesus also prayed passionately for the will of God to be done in His life.

Who in the days of his flesh, when he had offered up prayers and supplications with strong crying and tears unto him that was able to save him from death, and was heard in that he feared;

Hebrews 5:7

The evidence of this was when His "...sweat was as it were great drops of blood falling down to the ground" (Luke 22:44). Fervent prayer always works.

The ministry of Jesus was a great success! Two thousand years after these prayers, churches are still being started, books are still being written, songs are being composed about Christ, and more people are volunteering their lives to the service of our great God.

You will have great success in your ministry when you learn how to pray fervently. **Whenever you do not know what to do, do what Jesus did!** Jesus shouted when He prayed! (Hebrews 5:7). He prayed until He was sweating! Read it for yourself!

And being in an agony he prayed more earnestly: and his sweat was as it were great drops of blood falling down to the ground.

Luke 22: 44

You are coming out of barrenness today!

Now there were in the church that was at Antioch certain prophets and teachers; as Barnabas, and Simeon that was called Niger, and Lucius of Cyrene, and Manaen, which had been brought up with Herod the tetrarch, and Saul. As they ministered to the Lord, and fasted, the Holy Ghost said, Separate me Barnabas and Saul for the work whereunto I have called them. And when they had fasted and prayed, and laid their hands on them, they sent them away. So they, being sent forth by the Holy Ghost, departed unto Seleucia; and from thence they sailed to Cyprus.

Acts 13:1-4

The ministries of Paul and Barnabas were born out of intercession. The ministries of these two great men of God in New Testament times were born as they ministered unto the Lord and fasted. A praying church will always lead to new ministries and church growth. The way out of barrenness is the way into ministry. It is the way into evangelism. I believe that fervent prayer will almost always lead to fruitfulness in a minister's life. *A prayerful church almost always becomes fruitful.* Churches are born and ministers are sent out when real prayer begins.

Mysterious prayer will be the power that will break through the mysterious restrictions and barriers that hold you back from your fruitfulness.

Conclusion

It is my prayer that you will rise out of every form of barrenness that afflicts you. You will become a fruitful tree in the house of the Lord! No kind of barrenness will be associated with you after today!

To the making of many books there is no end! By these few words, receive encouragement and become a fruitful tree.

Amma

The Most Powerful Spiritual Light the World Has Ever Known

Ethan Walker III

Amma – The Most Powerful Spiritual Light the World Has Ever Known

Ethan Walker III

Address all enquiries to:

Devi Press
info@devipress.com

ISBN: 978-0-9987242-4-9

First edition – first printing
July, 2018
Printed in the United States

Cover graphic of Amma: Patty de Palacios

Pax Hominibus

I wish I could show you, when you are lonely or in darkness, the astonishing light of your own being.
- *Hafiz*

This book is dedicated to the unfolding blossom of light and love that lives and breathes in every heart. Your author humbly bows before his guru - Amma - who is an incarnation of Love and without whom this book could not have been written.

Contents

Introduction

This has been a difficult book to write. There are no words to describe the spiritual magnitude of Amma. To say that she is the most profound and most powerful and most compassionate of all the embodied saints, sages and buddhas the world has ever seen can easily be viewed as a bombastic claim. To say this is like dropping a big rock in the middle of the pond of our mind. We might as well have said aliens have landed on the Whitehouse Lawn and have asked to see the President!

To make this claim immediately invokes cognitive dissonance because it is so huge and would require significant reordering in our belief systems. Because of this, the mind will resist the notion that Amma is the most profound spiritual phenomenon ever to occur on the planet. It is your author's intent to show that after all is said in this book, these claims are still not big enough.

It should be noted as early as possible that Amma makes no such claims and would dismiss this discussion as meaningless prattle. Knowing that he runs the risk of being a prattler, your author continues unabated and compelled by the mind-blowing, white-hot sparks and shards of Amma's incomprehensible compassion that continue to shower us with penetrating cosmic grace; with love that is greater than the entire universe. The world desperately needs to understand who it is and what it is that now walks in their presence as Mata Amritanandamayi (Mother of Immortal Bliss).

Claiming that Amma is the Queen of the Universe is not meant to dismiss all of the other great saints and incarnations such as Jesus, Buddha and Krishna. It is only to say that what she is and what she has done, by far eclipses the lives of these spiritual luminaries.

Amma is the Queen of the Universe because she is an exceedingly powerful and brilliant incarnation of the Divine Mother – the creatrix of all that is. There have been other incarnations of the Divine Mother (including Jesus, Buddha and Krishna) but not with the power and intensity that has manifested through Amma.

An incarnation of tremendous power is necessary at this time because the darkness in the minds of mankind is so great.

3

Your author is well aware that making such claims will cause many to roll their eyes because we have heard this so many times from other religions. Jesus is the only way. Buddhism is the highest path on the planet. Krishna is greater than Shiva, no Shiva is greater than Krishna. And so it goes. However, this claim that Amma is the greatest ever is inclusive. It does not say Amma is the only way but we will say that all ways and all paths are part of the Divine Mother and Amma is that Divine Mother.

This view of oneness and unity could be made for any other truly self-realized Master. **The difference is the power with which this Truth manifests.**

We are considering the effect Amma is having or has had on the world and its inhabitants. The difference is between a 1 watt light bulb and a 1,000 watt light bulb. Even though the electricity (God/consciousness) in both is the same, the effect is much greater in the 1,000 watt bulb. 1 watt of love and compassion or 1,000 watts of love and compassion.

There are many Masters who are like boats that can carry us across the ocean of *Samsara* (seemingly endless rounds of births and deaths dogged by suffering at every turn).   By comparison, Amma is an ocean liner.

Amma Is Love

If we could for but a brief moment glimpse or grasp the immense love that Amma embodies we would go up in flames (good flames). We would be convinced beyond all doubt from this alone that Amma is who this book says she is. And this is a problem for most of us because most of us are aliens to love. We have experienced very little of it. We were born into a world in which there is almost no love and so we have not learned to love. Our parents never told us how important it is to cultivate love. We live in a desert which is dry and barren of love.

There are little sparks of it here and there – a mother and her child; our beloved dog or cat. But for the most part we have rocks for hearts and love is no more than a four-letter word. Because of this we can hear someone say, "Amma is love incarnate" and it has no more than a dry, intellectual meaning.

To really get this – to be swept up in the fires of love – to shed copious hot streaming tears of immense bliss and love – we have to sit in Amma's presence and often it does not happen the first time. There is no radiance of love on this planet that is greater than Amma. Amma truly is love incarnate and she is manifesting love in a very powerful way. We might recall John telling us in the New Testament that God *is* love (1 John 4:8).

But who in this world places any value on love?

Jubilee Amma

At the time of Jesus there was a practice among the Jewish people to grant pardons and forgive debts for no reason. This occurred every 50 years and was known as the *Jubilee*. It was a brief period when the door to liberation opened and those afflicted could walk through without having had to do anything to earn this freedom. According to the book of *Leviticus*, prisoners and slaves would be freed, debts would be forgiven, and the mercies of God would be visited upon the people.

Amma is like this. She is a cosmic jubilee. There is a Cosmic Mind which your author refers to as the Divine Mother of the Universe or just Divine Mother but one can also call it God, Our Father, Brahman, Buddha Nature, Allah, Great Spirit or any other name that one finds endearing.

When one begins to grasp the breathtakingly profound reality that is Amma - when the opportunity is realized - one will then be motivated to seize the moment and do whatever is necessary to walk through the door that is Amma. This is Jesus' parable of the *Pearl of Great Price*. Once the pearl is found, one sells all one has in order to purchase it. In other words, one abandons the toys and distractions of the world to swim in the ocean of bliss.

Even if one is not ready to walk out of their self-imposed prison, the Amma story, as a profoundly significant phenomenon, is well worth investigating. One can benefit from this as well because simply studying her, will change us for the better.

It should be understood by the reader that this book represents the opinions of your author and does not necessarily reflect the opinions of anyone else including Amma's official organization. Amma would never claim to be great in any way. Her humility is impeccable. But then that is one of the conditions that makes her so great!

To Declare or Not to Declare

Swami Paramatmananda, in one of his talks, describes the discussion he had with Swami Amritaswarupananda who wrote Amma's original biography. The discussion revolved around whether or not to declare Amma to be simply a hugging saint or an incarnation of the Divine – an avatar. Should they hold back on this information thus keeping the veil in place?

The idea is that making bold claims about being an incarnation might become an obstacle for some people. They would say, "Yeah, yeah, everyone says their guru is God!" They decided not to make any claims in the biography and allow the story of Amma's life to speak for itself. Those who have eyes to see will see and those that have ears to hear will hear.

It has been 30 plus years later and your author has observed many people not being able to pick up all the flowers of Amma's greatness so as to hold them all at once as a large bouquet thus realizing the magnitude of Amma's presence on this earth. We see that she has hugged 35 million people or feeds 10 million people a year or passes out spiritual experiences like candies or manifests great yogic supernormal powers but we never step back and look at all of these magnificent and luminous accomplishments as a whole. And so, it is with the intention of assembling the entire bouquet that your author embarks on this project.

For those who catch the scent from reading this book and want to dig more deeply into the profound mystery that is Amma, it is suggested to proceed to Amma's biography by Swami Amritaswarupananda. This is the best introduction for any who wish to understand Amma. It can be purchased at:

www.theammashop.org/books.

Your author also recommends reading *On the Road to Freedom* volume 2 by Swami

9

Paramatmananda available at the same online bookstore.

In addition, there are several excellent documentaries about Amma that can be viewed for free on YouTube® by searching for "River of Love Mata," "Science of Compassion," "Darshan the Embrace," and "Embracing the World." The last one is about Amma's charitable activities for serving the poor, the sick and the elderly. These can also be ordered as DVDs from www.theammashop.org.

Your author has put up an unofficial web site about Amma which presents her life and teachings. Go to www.ammaguide.com. The official websites for Amma are www.amma.org and www.amritapuri.org.

This book is an expression of the opinions of your author and are not necessarily the official stated positions of Amma's organization.

I humbly bow to Amma. She is my teacher and my guru and the reader is invited to explore my autobiography *Into the Mystic* to see the profound impact she has had on my life. Without her grace, this book could not have been written.

What Does Amma Claim?

It is important, as a first point in our investigation, that we explore the attitude Amma has regarding her own spiritual status. To begin with, Amma says in the *Awaken Children* books that the idea "I am spiritual" is a detriment to our own spiritual progress. So how does she respond to the inevitable inquiries regarding her divine nature?

Amma does not claim to be anything other than a normal human being. We will see from our investigation that she is anything but normal. This is what she says about any claim to being Divine.

"Questioner: Amma, do you claim anything?

Amma: Claim what?

Q: That you are an incarnation of the Divine Mother or a fully Self-realized Master and so forth.

A: Does the president or prime minister of any country keep on announcing, "Do you know who I am? I am the president/prime minister," wherever he or she goes? No.

11

They are what they are. Even to claim that you are an Avatar or are Self-realized involves ego. In fact, if somebody claims that they are an Incarnation, a Perfect Soul, that in itself is proof they are not.

Perfect Masters have no such claims. They always set an example to the world by being humble. Remember, Self-realization doesn't make you special. It makes you humble.

In order to claim that you are something, you neither have to be Self-realized nor do you need any special skill. The only thing that you need is a big ego, false pride. That is what a Perfect Master doesn't have." From the book *From Amma's Heart*

Amma typically responds to suggestions that she is enlightened, an avatar or a self-realized soul by dismissing it and laughing about it. Here are examples from the *Awaken Children* books:

"Brahmacharin (monk): (With joy) Now it is clear. Now I understand that Mother is an Avatar.

Amma: (Laughing and rejoicing) No, no... your Mother is not an Avatar but a good-for-nothing crazy girl."

And

"She laughed and replied, "To this crazy one? Shiva! Mother is mad, a nut!"

And

"Mother: Children, what does Mother know? Mother is crazy. She would simply say some crazy things. Siva! Siva! Children, accept what you think is correct."

Amma the Astonishing Light

We wish to explore the idea that Amma (Mata Amritanandamayi) is the greatest spiritual presence to ever appear on this earth in recorded history. This is a bold claim and yet it can be proven to be true to anyone who takes the time to investigate.

What do we mean by great? Here is the short list.

- Unfathomable river of unconditional love
- Manifestation of unparalleled compassion
- Selfless actions
- Spotless humility
- Spiritual transmission to tens of thousands
- Profound miracles
- Frequent immersion in Samadhi or ecstatic states
- Merged in the Divine Mother while still a teenager
- In possession of all divine powers while still a teenager
- All of this with no guru or teacher

Kali Yuga

The earth is now at a peak point of darkness – the peak of the Kali Yuga. Dark qualities such as self-centered obsessions, absence of love and compassion, greed, arrogance, addictions and absorption in the unbridled pursuit of pleasures at the expense of others, have gripped the minds of human kind.

When darkness has engulfed the world, there appears a concentrated focus of light as a balance. This is Amma. That is not to say there are not other spiritual beings on this planet at this time who yield considerable light. And there have been great Masters in the past – Buddha, Jesus, Padmasambhava, Krishna. It is the opinion of your author that none of these are as great as Amma in terms of radiating spiritual power, light and love and changing the hearts of people. No one has done so much for so many in such a short amount of time. No one has sacrificed as much as Amma for the upliftment of humanity.

It is possible that there have been beacons of light equal to or greater than the phenomenon we know as Amma, but they were reclusive and hidden and we have no record of them.

Amma is an astonishingly powerful incarnation of the Divine Mother of the Universe. She is the most powerful incarnation of the Divine Mother in the history of the world. *Divine Mother* is a term used here to describe the primordial energy of Shakti from which the universe arises. She is also Brahman the changeless primordial awareness. And she is the eternal Cosmic Mind that orchestrates the eternally changing. The Divine Mother, as presented in this book, is the *all in all*. The reader is invited to substitute any other descriptive handle to envision the *all in all*.

What we see as Amma is really a mask that the Divine Mother has put on for the purpose of helping her children.

It is not easy to see behind the mask that is Amma. This requires *punya* or spiritual merit that has been garnered from past lives doing spiritual practices, serving a Master, expressing deep compassion with acts of caring and so on. Punya from past lives is required to even have mild curiosity about the spiritual path in this life. Those who have no interest have no punya. To recognize Amma's profound magnitude requires a lot of punya. Thus, not many people will be able to see Amma this way even when confronted with the many articles of her greatness. They will simply be blind to it. Even people with spiritual interest and meditating for years will not be able to recognize Amma because her light is so brilliant. Because her light is so great, the opportunity to benefit by merely being in her presence is also very great. Thus, their karma, their insufficient punya, will not allow them to recognize Amma.

If one is fortunate enough to see Amma as the Divine Mother herself, then one should drop everything else and camp on Amma's doorstep metaphorically speaking. This is not to berate any other path such as devotion to Jesus or Buddha, but these will always be there and we can come back to them later after Amma leaves the body. We can even stay on any other path and still embrace Amma as an incarnation of the Divine.

To actually have the Divine Mother incarnate among us is exceedingly rare and equally fortuitous for those who have the eyes to see. It is a blessing beyond anything else available on the planet today. It is a blessing beyond anything else that has been available in the recorded history of human kind.

Suppose it is 2,000 or so years ago and Jesus is alive and teaching. Or picture Buddha or Krishna if one likes. If we had the good fortune to recognize him as an incarnation, we would drop everything and spend as much time with him as possible. Imagine if we had the ability to see into the past and know that we were there but did not take advantage. We did not follow him in his mission. We did not hear the *Sermon on the Mount* because relatives were coming to our house to visit that day. We would marvel that we could not have seen the importance of the Master's presence and what an extremely rare opportunity it was to be with him. Had we seen it, we would have asked our relatives to pick another day. And then, just like that, he was gone.

Exhibits of Greatness

The first place to look is Amma's biography. Reading this is highly recommended for any who wish to understand Amma.

From a very young age, Amma was absorbed in the Divine in the form of Krishna. She would

dance with him, talk to him, meditate and carry on this way all through the night.

Amma would care for and feed the poor, sick and elderly often being beaten by her parents for giving away family food and jewelry (her family was very poor and her father was a fisherman).

By the time she was a teenager, she was in possession of all yogic powers (levitation, bilocation, divine healing, reading other's thoughts etc.). The biography presents many instances of the use of these divine powers including bringing the dead back to life. Siddhis (powers) do not indicate enlightenment although most if not all incarnations have them. What is of interest here is that she attained these powers while still a teenager without the help of any teacher or guru.

While still a teenager, the Divine Mother of the Universe merged in her. From that time on, Amma saw nothing as separate from her Self. This is such a young age for such occurrences and underscores the extraordinary divinity of Amma's being.

To follow is an excerpt from *A Biography of Mata Amritanandamayi* by Swami Amritaswarupananda describing this.

"Her voice became choked. Her breathing stopped completely. Sudhamani (young Amma) fell unconscious. The Will of the Mother designates the moment. The Divine Enchantress of the Universe, the Omniscient, the Omnipresent, the Omnipotent Being, the Ancient, Primal Creatrix, the Divine Mother, appeared before Sudhamani in a living form dazzling like a thousand suns. Sudhamani's heart overflowed in a tidal wave of unspeakable love and bliss. The Divine Mother benignly smiled, and, becoming a Pure Effulgence, merged in Sudhamani.

"The divine event is best described in Sudhamani's own composition, *Ananda Veethi* or *The Path of Bliss*, in which she has tried to make intelligible that mystical union which is beyond words :

Ananda Veethi

"Once upon a time,
   my soul was dancing
In delight

through the Path of Bliss.
At that time,
  all the inner foes such as
Attraction and aversion
  ran away, hiding
Themselves in the innermost
  recesses of my mind.

Forgetting myself,
  I merged in a golden dream
Which arose within me.
As noble aspirations
Clearly manifested themselves
  in my mind,
The Divine Mother,
  with bright, gentle hands,
Caressed my head.
With bowed head, I told Mother
  that my life is dedicated to Her.

Smiling, She became
  a Divine Effulgence
And merged in me.
  My mind blossomed,
Bathed in the many-hued
  Light of Divinity
And the events

of millions of years gone by
Rose up within me.
Thenceforth, seeing nothing
   as separate from my own Self
A single Unity, and merging in
   the Divine Mother,
I renounced all sense of enjoyment.

Mother told me to ask the people
To fulfil their human birth.
Therefore, I proclaim
   to the whole world
The sublime Truth
   that She uttered,
"Oh man, merge in your Self!"

Thousands and thousands of yogis
Have taken birth in India
and lived the principles
   visualized by the Great Sages
   of the unknown past.
To remove the sorrow
   of humanity,
How many naked truths there are!

Today I tremble with bliss
Recollecting Mother's words,
"Oh my darling, come to Me,

Leaving all other works.
You are always Mine."

O Pure Consciousness,
O Embodiment of Truth,
I will heed Your words.

O Mother, why are You late in coming?
Why did You give this birth?
I know nothing, O Mother,
Please forgive my mistakes."

Absorbed in Ecstasy

Through her late teens, 20s and into her 30s Amma's mind would spontaneously ascend into the stratosphere of the Divine and she would lose outer consciousness. **This would happen on an almost daily basis!** As she grew older she was more able to control her mind and keep it in the empirical plane.

Amma's mind is like a balloon she has to hold under the water of the material world – it is constantly wanting to shoot up. Imagine having to struggle every day to stay out of the Cosmic! There have been no other saints of this magnitude in the history of human kind.

> "Even now I am struggling hard to keep my mind down, especially while singing bhajans. It is always shooting up." Amma, *Awaken Children*, vol. 1

After being asked about her divine moods, Amma recounts her struggle to remain conscious in the world:

> Amma: (Abstractedly) "Oh...I don't know. They just come like that. (After a short pause) Do you know how much I am struggling to stay here in this world in the midst of all of you? It is really very difficult. But when Mother remembers the sorrows and sufferings of the people, Her mind melts and becomes compassionate. That is what keeps Her mind down here." As told by Swami Amritaswarupananda, *Awaken Children, vol. 2.* Amma often talks about herself in the third person.

To follow is a description of one such event.

Struggling to Stay Down

"At six-thirty in the evening the residents began the singing of bhajans. After a few songs, Brahmacharin Balu started singing Saranagati (O Mother, Give Refuge). By the time the Holy Mother came to join in, the same song was still being sung since it was a long bhajan. She took over the lead singing.

"O Light that illumines the whole Universe And even the sun, moon and the stars; O Primordial Nature, Governess of the entire Universe, O Universal Mother, who is the Incarnation Of pure and selfless Love, this destitute cries for Thy vision with a heart endowed with intense yearning.

"The Mother was unusually enraptured with the bliss of Divine Love. She swayed vigorously from side to side, back and forth. An inexpressible and indescribably beautiful blending of the diverse aspects of supreme devotion and love slowly manifested in the Mother. It enveloped each and every person present. Through the Divine voice of the Holy Mother the song attained wings. It soared up

27

and flowed like a never-ending stream as the song continued:

"O Mother, the ocean sings Thy Glory Through the resounding of the Sacred Syllable, Aum...one after the other, Each and every wave dances gleefully In time with the Pranava, the Primordial Sound, Aum...

"With a voice full of feeling and a heart full of longing, the Mother called out, "Amme...Amme..." Her eyes were fixed on the sky above and her hands were out-stretched. The Mother's call was so full of love and authenticity that it gave the feeling to everyone that the Divine Mother Herself was standing in front of the Holy Mother. The Mother sang out,

"O Mother Divine, Thou art beyond The scriptural verses of Purushasuktha (Scriptural text which glorifies the Universal Being).

"O Mother, Thou art beyond the Brahmasutra (Scriptural text which describes the Absolute Brahman).

"O Mother, even transcending all the four Vedas,

"O Mother, Thou alone knowest Thee indeed.

"At this point the Mother started laughing, an external expression of her inner bliss. This mysterious laughter persisted as the brahmacharins continued singing. The Mother clapped her hands like a little child and immediately raised both hands above her head. Now the laughter stopped, but her hands remained in the uplifted position for a while. The fingers of each hand displayed two different divine mudras. A beatific glow illumined her face. Bringing her hands down, the Mother again sang:

"O Mother, seeking Thee, this child will cry, Wandering along the shores of many seas; O Mother, to each and every particle of sand This child inquires about Thee. O stars, glittering in the vast blue sky,

Did any one of you see my Mother
Passing through this way?

"The Mother sang these lines repeatedly, over
and over again. The shawl which covered her
head had fallen down as Gayatri tried to place
it back into position. Strands of her hair fell
loose around her neck and gently swirled
around as her head swayed with the rhythm
of the music. Tears trickled down her cheeks.
Raising her hands up, the Mother went on
calling, "Amma... Amma... Amma..." This
went on until finally she burst into a flood of
tears, but the next moment the Mother took a
long, deep breath and became still. Her hands
still manifested divine mudras. The
brahmacharins went on singing,

"O my Mother Bhairavi, there is no shore
Where I have not searched for Thee,
O Mother, my darling Mother,
Bliss-embodied One, No time exists when I
have not sought for Thee, O my Beloved
Mother, for aeons and aeons Hast Thou hid
from me, This poor child of Thine.
O Compassionate One, why dost Thou delay
To shower Thy Grace upon this child?

"In the light of the burning oil lamp everyone could see the radiant face of the Holy Mother. No sign of external consciousness was evident. Saturated with divinity, the atmosphere evoked spontaneous meditation in the minds of all who were present, devotees and residents alike. One could easily discern that they were all singing with their minds fully fixed on the object of their meditation. Some sang with their minds totally focused on their Beloved Deity, shedding tears of bliss, while others sat unmoving, deeply absorbed in profound meditation. Struggling to bring her mind down to the physical plane of consciousness, the Holy Mother once again sang,

"O Mother, On Thy fingertips revolve hundreds, Nay, millions of universes; How is it justified if Thou makest me, This poor child, also revolve on the same fingertips of Thine?

"Again the Mother was transported to her own world of infinite bliss. She lost her control to stay in this physical plane and stood up. As she walked towards the coconut grove in her ecstatic rapture, she allowed herself to drown completely in the ocean of love and supreme devotion. Such was her God-intoxicated state. Spell-bound, the brahmacharins and devotees continued to glorify the Divine Mother as they sang,

O Mother, come to me, Stand in front of me today; I wish to inundate Thy Holy Feet with my tears. O Mother, the sound that rings in my heart, The emergent tune from my heart Is the call of loving devotion unto Thee. O Mother, other than that, I need nothing...

"The bhajan ended with these lines. Enjoying the experience of bliss and the fervor of pure devotion and love, everyone sat immersed in meditation. Total silence prevailed, the silence of inner peace. This hallowed atmosphere hung suspended in a sacred stillness as the cool, gentle breeze floated the beckoning call of the ocean from the west.

"After the arati, everyone's eyes and hearts reached out in search of the Holy Mother. Standing at a respectful distance, they all watched the Mother dancing in pure bliss. It felt as if the Mother was dancing all around the entire Ashram even though she was only encircling that one particular spot in the coconut grove. Completely lost to this external world in which we were standing, she reveled in her own mystical inundation of splendor." *Swami Amirtaswarupananda,* Awaken Children*, vol. III, p. 261*

Your author knows only of one other saint in recent history that had difficulty keeping their mind from soaring into the ocean of bliss and that was Sri Ramakrishna (1836–1886). His experiences were not nearly as frequent as Amma's and he did 16 years of intense spiritual practice to get to that point.

Amma gave instructions to her renunciate (monks and nuns) children to sing and chant certain mantras when her mind went into the Cosmic. She explained that there was a possibility that if they failed to do this she might not come back.

All of this was available to Amma while a teenager and beyond with no instruction or help from anyone. No guru assisted Amma. In fact, she had intense opposition and harassment from her own family and the "rationalists" in the village. A woman, and especially a young girl, is forbidden from touching other men so her hugging darshans deeply violated the cultural morays of the time.

In Indian culture, there are no public displays of physical affection even among married people. Amma would walk down the pathways and avenues accompanied by the most profane insults and the hurling of rocks. Because of Amma's activities, all of her relatives, aunts, uncles and so on, blacklisted Amma's parents and siblings. All alone in the world, and against intense opposition, Amma conquered all.

Her deep ecstatic states, wherein she lost consciousness of the empirical world, continued on an almost daily basis. While those of us in pursuit of the Divine long to have even one such cosmic experience, Amma struggled in the opposite direction to stay *out* of the Divine so she could serve ailing humanity. Imagine such a thing! This is utterly without precedent.

Here is another ecstatic, blissful absorption in the Divine from *Awaken Children* by Swami Amritaswarupananda:

"The sound of the ocean waves served as background accompaniment to Mother's song, and soon She was again lost in a mood of divine rapture. She laughed and smiled as tears rolled down Her cheeks. Raising both Her hands, the Mother sang. As Mother Herself has said, Her mind is always spontaneously shooting up to the highest plane of consciousness.

"Within a split second She can switch off this world of plurality, this world of names and forms, and travel towards the unknown. Just like a child who can go to the kitchen and obtain the message needed for the stranger waiting in the sitting room, Mother can ascend and descend any time She wishes. Mother has free access to both worlds. We onlookers see only the closing and opening of Her eyes, the circling of Her hand, the uttering of Namah Sivaya or a blissful laughing, but we know nothing about the incomprehensible Supreme Reality where She is constantly established." *Awaken Children*, Swami Amritaswarupananda

Here is another account of one of Amma's ecstatic moods. There are many of them described in Amma's biography and in the *Awaken Children* series of books.

"The evening bhajan started as usual at six-thirty. The singing reached its peak as the Holy Mother sang,

O Beautiful One, please come,

O Consort of Purandara (Lord Siva), please come,

O Auspicious One, please come...

O Giver of radiance,

Thou art the All in all of those

Who consider Thee as their dear relation...

O Mother, please remain as the spring of my inspiration...

"Becoming intoxicated with God-love and, standing up, the Mother began dancing ecstatically. The brahmacharins went on singing with overflowing devotion. From the temple verandah the Mother moved towards the coconut trees in the front yard. When She reached the coconut trees She danced round and round completely lost to this world. She was showing a divine gesture (mudra) with Her right hand which was slightly raised.

"A beaming smile lit Her face which was clear even in the dim light. This ecstatic mood had gone on for more than half an hour and it seemed as though there would be no end to it. Some sat nearby and others at a distance watching the Mother. Some of the brahmacharins made a chain by holding hands to protect Mother from hitting the coconut trees.

"Eventually Sugunanandan, because of his usual fear that his daughter would leave Her body soon if this state persisted for a long time, appeared on the scene. Without asking anybody's permission, he carried Her into the hut and laid Her on a cot. Mother was totally lost to this world and Her body now seemed like a corpse. Sugunanandan later related, "The little one's body was so light in weight that it felt like I was lifting a basketful of flowers, but Her face was glowing like the rising sun." *Swami Amritaswarupananda, Awaken Children, vol. 1, p. 118*

Ramakrishna comments that *Prema* or ecstatic love is absolutely the highest state of spirituality:

> The first stage of spiritual practice is association with spiritual people, the company of holy men. The second stage is faith in things relating to the Spirit. The third stage is single-minded devotion to one's Ideal. The Ideal may be one's Guru, the spiritual teacher, the Impersonal Brahman, the Personal God or any of His manifestations. The fourth stage is the state of being struck speechless at the thought of God. The fifth stage, when the feeling of devotion to God reaches the highest point; it is called *Mahabhava*. The devotee sometimes laughs, sometimes weeps like a madman. He loses all control over his body. This state is not attained by ordinary human beings who are not capable of conquering the flesh. It is reached by Incarnations of God who appear in this world for the salvation of mankind. The sixth stage, *Prema* or ecstatic love, goes hand in hand with Mahabhava. It is the most

intense love of God and is strictly the highest state of spirituality. The two marks of this stage are the forgetfulness of this world and the forgetfulness of self, which includes one's own body. *Gospel of Ramakrishna,* translated by Swami Abhedananda

Amma shows the fifth and sixth stages of Divine Love which are only accessed by incarnations of the Divine.

Miracles

So many miracles have happened with Amma! It is best to read the biography to feel the full import of this. Amma herself downplays miracles and the use of supernormal powers that are available to yogis. She says that siddhis (powers) are equal to excreta.

Most people who have been following Amma for a length of time have miracles of their own to recount including your author. What is important to see, is that Amma wielded these powers at a very young age – while still a teenager without the help of any teacher or guru.

Here are some of them. You can read about these in Amma's biography and also in the condensed book *A Pilgrim's Guide to Amma*.

Knowing the Minds of Others

Levitation

Death and Resurrection of Her Own Body

Materialization

Bi-location

Talking to Subtle Beings

Perfume Smell

Fire Balls

Healing

Raising People from the Dead

Predicting the Future

Dispensing Divine Births

Going Without Sleep

The Divine Hug

This is the first phenomenon that most people notice that would not be possible for a normal human being. Your author does not know of any other hugging saints either now or in the history of humankind. This is perhaps her most miraculous and astonishing accomplishment.

To date it is estimated that Amma has hugged 35 million people. It is almost meaningless to make such a statement because we can't conceive of 35 million people.   We know it's a lot but that's about it. One has to watch Amma do this in order to begin to appreciate the magnitude of it.

To put this in perspective, Amma has been hugging for 40 plus years but in the early days the crowds were small. So we will call it 40. 35,000,000 people divided by 40 gives us 875,000 people hugged on average each year. Divide this again by 365 days in a year and she averages 2,397 hugs a day. Of course, she doesn't hug every day. When she is at the ashram, she hugs 4 days a week. Out on tour she hugs maybe 5 or 6 days a week with no rest in between stops except to travel. She tours extensively in India and it is common to hug 10 thousand in one day.

It will be of interest to search YouTube for "Amma darshan" in order to see Amma do this. If we attempted such a hugging feat, we would become bored, despondent from listening to tragic stories with pleas for help and we would tire of lifting our arm to embrace each person after doing so 100 or 200 times. Imagine doing this for 10 or 12 hours day after day! And for 40 years! And for free!

In the USA she starts hugging at 10 am and continues until maybe 3 pm. In the evening at 7:30 pm, there is a program of talks and singing bhajans led by Amma. Then she starts hugging at around 10 pm and will finish at maybe 3 am. Then it starts again the next day. In between cities there is usually a day with no hugging.

If we stay up with Amma until the early hours of the morning we can see at the end she is still bright, fresh, laughing, joking and using the same amount of deep concentration on each person as with the beginning of the hugging session hours earlier. No normal human being could ever do this.

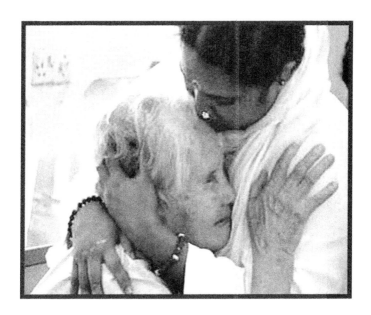

Most saints and holy people decline to touch others because it dissipates the spiritual energy of the saint. There is a passage in the Bible where Jesus is in a crowd and a woman touches him.

> "And Jesus said, "Who is the one who touched Me?" And while they were all denying it, Peter said, "Master, the people are crowding and pressing in on You." But Jesus said, "Someone did touch Me, for I was aware that power had gone out of Me." *Luke* 8:46

He spins around and asks the disciples who had touched him because the "energy" or "virtue" had gone out of him. If one touch caused so much concern for Jesus, what are we to think of Amma who not only touches but hugs millions? Can we begin to grasp the unfathomable power Amma wields to perform such an enormous act of unbridled compassion? Jesus was drained after a single touch!

The first question we must ask is what would motivate someone to hug day and night for 40 plus years and ask nothing in return. There is no cost of admission. The answer is Amma's love and compassion compels her to do this. What other reason can there be? It is not for

money as Amma lives in a small, sparsely appointed flat at the ashram. Besides, most people would not could not do this for any amount of money! How big would such a love be to motivate a person to hug 35 million people?

While the evidence we see before us points to love and compassion, we are unable to grasp the magnitude of such a love. We are dumbstruck as we begin to reckon with it.

In the USA this goes non-stop from late May until late July. In Europe the crowds are generally twice as big as in the USA. In India it is common for 10 thousand people to line up each day for a hug!

On many occasions, Amma has hugged for 14 to 16 hours straight and on a few occasions, she has hugged for 24 hours without stopping. Imagine hugging for 24 hours without ever having food or using the bathroom! When Amma hugs, she closes her eyes and concentrates deep within our psyche. She heals and purifies past wounds even going back multiple lifetimes.

Swami Amritaswarupananda (one of Amma's senior swamis) has this to say about Amma's hugs:

"Amma's darshan is a healing process, a wonderful divine healing process. Her touch heals the wounds caused by a painful past. Her presence purifies, uplifts, and carries us toward our true Self. Amma is purity embodied. Thus all those who come in contact with Her are transformed and cleansed. In some cases, this purification can be seen, while at other times, it is subtle. How many of Amma's devotees are familiar with the seemingly innocent hug that transforms lives, and with the look that causes hearts to melt.

Whether you are aware of it or not, whether or not you feel worthy, this purification happens. Just as an iron piece is magnetized when it is rubbed constantly by a powerful magnet, an ordinary soul is transformed into a spiritual being through the constant contact and companionship of a Mahatma like Amma." *Awaken Children, vol. 7*

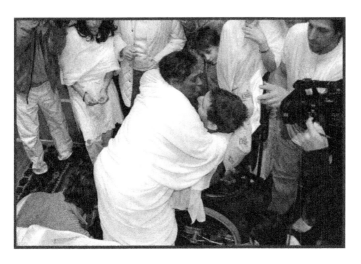

The Divine energy that pours out of Amma is quite astonishing. A word commonly used to describe this energy is Shakti (primordial energy as the first emanation from the formless Absolute – there has never been a time that there was no Shakti – it is without beginning or end).

Most anyone can feel Amma's immense unconditional love and boundless compassion. Many people, when they are close to Amma, feel an actual heat on the chest and face. Many report that after a hug their bodies feel like they are vibrating in a most pleasant way. Still others are smitten with bliss and it is all they can do to make it to a chair and sit until the experience passes. Many weep with tears of deep and profound joy.

Most people comment after their first hug that they felt Amma loved them more than their own mother. One feels very accepted and loved in Amma's presence. All fear and apprehension dissolve like mist in the morning sun.

51

Spiritual Transmissions

Along with these hugs, Amma has given out many thousands of spiritual experiences. This alone is quite astonishing and is perhaps her most magnificent gift of grace. Your author has experienced these on a number of occasions.

The scope and intensity of these transmissions can vary. For some, Amma puts them into a state of non-duality or pure witnessing lasting a few hours or a few days. Others may dissolve into the Divine Light. Visions and knowledge of the Divine Mother or visions of Amma as Jesus or Kali are common. One may be overcome with intense love and devotion for the Divine or for Amma shedding rivers of tears swimming in the ocean of cosmic bliss.

Swami Paramatmananda recounts in his book *On the Road to Freedom, volume 1*, an experience that occurred only a few days after arriving at Amma's hermitage for the first time. He had been suffering from severe health problems for many years.

"That night was Darshan. I remained in the temple for as long as I could during both the Bhavas. I felt the atmosphere within the temple charged with spiritual peace. Meditation came with very little effort. I went and lay down behind the temple. I did not feel like going into the house. I wanted to be as near to Amma as possible. The Darshan was finishing and Chandru came to call me. He said that Devi (Amma) was calling me to come to the front of the temple. I came around to the front of the temple and stood facing her. Seeing me there, she walked briskly over to me and gave me an affectionate hug. Then bending down, she whispered into my ear, "My son, do not worry, your body will become better." She then slowly backed up into the temple and was standing in front of the door looking at me. As she was looking at me, I noticed that her face was getting brighter and brighter. Gradually, the brightness expanded so much that it engulfed her whole body and then the temple and even the surroundings. I could see nothing but that brilliant but soothing light. Suddenly the effulgence contracted to the size of a pinpoint, its brilliance making me squint. A moment later it stopped. I was once again seeing Amma smiling at me.   The temple doors were closed, and the Darshan ended."

Here is another example. A friend of your author's, we will call her Marty, was sitting in the hall while Amma was leading the singing of bhajans (devotional songs).   People were clapping and some were dancing on the sides. Marty then had the desire for everything to be quiet and still. Suddenly a beam of light shot out of Amma's heart and connected with Marty's heart. She rose out of her body to the top of the hall and everything was very quiet and peaceful. She describes the experience as being in the middle of a perfectly calm ocean. She could also see a rain of golden light falling everywhere in the hall blessing all in attendance. Marty was not a meditator and had had no other transcendental experiences. This was wholly by Amma's grace.

On another occasion, Amma put sandalwood paste in between your author's eyebrows. This resulted in a blissful state of being the pure witness of all that was occurring. This lasted for two days.

Another friend was sitting with your author listening to Amma lead the singing of bhajans in an evening program. He had his eyes closed and his hands were held straight out with his elbows at his sides and with the palms up. As he listened to and became absorbed in Amma's singing, he felt as if both hands had become connected to a very powerful current of blissful, divine energy. This put his mind in a very still and high plane of consciousness lasting for some time.

Another good friend says that each time Amma hugs her, she goes into a transcendental breathless state.

Yet another friend went to see Amma for the first time and on the first hug, Amma drew a circle between her eyebrows and wrote or marked something in the circle with the tip of Amma's finger. For the rest of the day, the friend felt she was totally one with Amma and was in a place of deep imperturbability.

The first time your author went to see Amma, she gave him the vision of the Divine Mother which has not only lasted to this day but has deepened and expanded as the result of doing practices suggested by Amma. This experience is described in detail in your author's autobiography *Into the Mystic*.

These spiritual transmissions from Amma are called *diksha* in Sanskrit. This is the transmission of spiritual energy or insight by a self-realized being to another and can happen by a glance, a touch or by silence. Normally, these experiences are rarely given by Masters to those who come to them. But Amma is the Divine Mother of the Universe and it is her way to bestow endless blessings on her children. This is the nature of a Mother. She is a cornucopia of spiritual experiences. She has strewn jewels of cosmic bliss and insight on the ground in front of us and we only have to pick them up. Such a powerful and fortuitous dispensation of grace is extremely rare and we should not pass up the opportunity to experience Amma's great light and benefit from it.

Another personal friend left his body upon being hugged by Amma. His hug was over but he could not move because he was hovering above his body! In short order he got his arms to work but his legs were still immovable. Attendants picked him up under the arms and set him beside Amma allowing a little time to pass so that he could completely reinter his body. He describes the experience as being very blissful and transcendent.

Amma gives us these experiences as a way of teaching. She gives us the experience of the Divine so we know how to direct the course of our spiritual path – that we will be inspired to persist. She is teaching us what it feels like otherwise we would have no inkling as to where we are going. She is giving us the carrot to motivate us. This is much better than being motivated by the whip of suffering!

Sri Ramakrishna died in 1886 at the age of 50. He had throat cancer. He stated that the cancer was the result of giving spiritual experiences to some people. He did not pass them out freely like Amma nor did he have even a small fraction of the crowds. He might have 20 people in his room on a good night maybe once or twice per week. It is your author's guess that perhaps in his whole life he gave spiritual experiences to 50 people. This is based on the frequency of such occasions in *The Gospel of Ramakrishna*. Ramakrishna commented that when he gave a spiritual experience, he had to accept into himself some of the person's karma. According to him, taking on these karmas eventually resulted in throat cancer.

How powerful is Amma who has given tens of thousands of these spiritual experiences!

Sitting in the Presence of Amma

The literary epic the *Ramayana* describes activities in the life of Rama who was an actual person who walked the earth - an incarnation of the Divine. Rama tells his brother Lakshman and his wife Sita why even sitting in the presence of these rare souls is such a blessing:

> Rama: These men of mystic powers live far from the world. They perform penance in this wilderness. They don't exhibit their powers in cities or towns. They are very rare beings. We benefit even by their mere presence.

> Sita: How does their mere presence benefit us?

> Rama: Sita, just as from merely sitting in the sun its warmth enters our bodies. Similarly, being in their physical presence the inner light of their spiritual knowledge, their subtly of emotion, permeates our inner core. Without many words they speak profound truths. To reap full benefit of their wisdom we must keep open the doors and windows of our mind and reside at their feet. If we go to them with all the humility of a beggar, and lay open our minds in receptive calm, the pearls garnered by their penance will be

given to you without your striving. Lakshman, only rare fortune gives one such opportunities. Even the sight of such great sages is rarely gained.

In the following quote from Amma, she further underscores this truth:

> Spiritual progress that cannot be had through pilgrimages and austerities (meditation, mantra japa, etc.) can be gained in the presence of mahatmas. We may be able to perform austerities for many years. But the presence of mahatmas is much harder to come by. That is why, if we get a chance to be in their presence, we should never throw it away. The benefits that cannot be gained even after performing austerities for 10 years can be gained from just one darshan or one touch of a mahatma. However, we should approach them without arrogance, but with humility and faith. Only then can we benefit from their presence. - Amma, *Awaken Children*

Ramana Maharshi comments on the advantage of being in the physical presence of a true Master:

"True, that in the proximity of a great master, the vasanas (mental tendencies) will cease to be active, the mind becomes still and samadhi results, similar to fire not scorching because of other devices. Thus, the disciple gains true knowledge and right experience in the presence of the master." *Ramana Maharshi, Talks with Sri Ramana Maharshi*

Below, Amma is leading the singing of bhajans (devotional songs). When a Mahatma or Self-realized being sings, the force of the light of the Absolute projects powerfully through their singing. In the picture below, the shaft of light is cosmic light caught by a camera. Your author has other photos like this and it is a phenomenon. You can see the exploding shaft of light is covering up the microphone stand, Amma's left arm and the top of Swamiji's head meaning they are positioned behind the light. The beam of cosmic light is coming out of the center of Amma's chest. One can see other wispy anomalies of light which are also typically seen.

Supernormal Powers

Amma's biography details many instances in which Amma has used supernormal powers known as *siddhis*.

> "A true Master never gives importance to siddhis. He has all the powers needed under his sway. Even then, he will always remain simple and humble." *Amma, Awaken Children, vol 1*

Spiritual powers are not an indication of spiritual greatness. However, divine incarnations – avatars – will be in possession of these powers. It is possible for an individual who is not Self-realized to attain such powers. Spiritual aspirants should avoid seeking siddhis as they will create ego and pride and ruin the aspirant.

Most everyone who has spent much time around Amma has experienced her omniscience at one time or another such as a clear indication that Amma had perceived our thoughts.

On one occasion, a woman from Yugoslavia was seeing Amma for the very first time. Upon her approach to Amma, Amma began singing a

Yugoslavian lullaby in the language of Yugoslavian which had been sung by the woman's mother when the woman was a child.

The author knows a couple who went to see Amma for the first time in Santa Fe. Let's call them Marvin and Sally. After a couple of hugs, Marvin was bitten with the not-worthy syndrome and decided he would not go up for any more hugs because, as he put it, he did not want to soil the Holy Mother's presence with his miserable wretched self. However, Sally was not having any of this and so she went for a hug without her partner. At the hug, Amma gave Sally two chocolate candy kisses. Normally, Amma gives each person one chocolate candy kiss. Sitting down by Marvin, Sally exclaimed, "See Marvin! Amma thinks you should have gotten a hug. She gave me two chocolates!" Marvin still could not overcome his self-loathing and would not believe what Sally was suggesting. At the end of the program, an isle formed for Amma to walk down as she exited the tent. Marvin was on the inside edge of this isle on his knees as Amma approached. Coming to Marvin, she stopped, bent over, looked at him squarely and holding up two fingers said, "Two chocolates!"

Levitation

In *Awaken Children* book 4 there is a description of Amma becoming the goddess Kali and levitating off the floor while sitting cross-legged. This she did for a holy man who was desirous of having the darshan of the goddess and was witnessed by a dozen or more people.

Death and Resurrection of Her Own Body

There is an instance of this described in the biography. Amma's father demanded that the Divine Mother give his daughter back to him. Amma replied that if she did, he would get only a corpse. Her father continued to insist and at that point Amma instantly fell over - stone dead. There was no pulse and no breathing. After some time, rigor mortis set in. There were many people witnessing this and there arose a great tumult of wailing, crying and grief. At the end of 8 hours, Amma's father was overcome with remorse and prayed sincerely through his tears to the Divine

Mother that She restore Amma to life. He promised never to interfere again. At that point Amma's body began to show signs of life and she fully recovered. She had been dead for 8 hours and was as stiff as a board with rigor mortis.

Materialization

There is an instance in which a very young Amma put her finger in a pitcher of water in the presence of a thousand or more persons and turned the water into pudding. It was then distributed to all the people gathered and the pitcher remained full the entire time. Described in Amma's biography.

Bi-location

This is the appearance of two flesh and blood Amma bodies in two places simultaneously. There are many descriptions of this in the *Awaken Children* books and the biography. In these she will appear and perform physical actions, maybe moving things or physically touch or caress an individual. Then when the recipient is next in front of Amma she will make a comment indicating her full awareness of the event.

Talking to Subtle Beings

In the biography, Amma was taking sewing lessons at a nearby Catholic Church. She describes sitting in the adjacent cemetery and conversing with the departed souls. She would enquire into their wellbeing and console them.

In 1987, during Amma's first visit to the USA, she was to give a program in Santa Fe. The morning after her first night there, she mentioned to her hosts that she had been up all night giving darshan to the most unusual beings. She then

proceeded to describe them. Her hosts produced a picture book of Kachinas (deities of local Native American Indians) and Amma verified those were the beings to whom she had been giving darshan.

Perfume Smell

Many followers of Amma have experienced the scent of rose and sandalwood that Amma wears. This can occur at anytime, anywhere and the fragrance will be quite strong. The author has experienced this on a number of occasions as have many followers of Amma.

Fire Balls

On at least two occasions, Amma created large moving fire balls to disperse crowds of hostile non-believers. This is described in Amma's biography.

Healing

Amma's healing events are very numerous. The author once gave a woman a ride to a program and she recounted that she had ovarian cancer. There was a tumor as big as a baseball in her abdomen and it was physically palpable by pressing with finger tips. It had once been removed surgically but had grown back. At the suggestion of a friend, the woman spent a weekend with Amma. The following Monday at her doctor's appointment, no trace of the tumor could be found.

One morning the author was ready to do morning meditations but his back between the shoulder blades was out and in so much pain he questioned that he could sit on the floor for any length of time. After settling in and closing his eyes, suddenly, and quite without any thought of this, Amma appeared in his mind's eye and said, "Son, does your back hurt? Here, let Amma fix it for you." She then reached over his shoulder and placed her palm on his back between the shoulder blades. The pain disappeared completely at that point and did not return. There are many thousands of stories like this among devotees.

There is a well-known occurrence of Dattan the leper appearing in the back of the shed where Amma was giving darshan (hugging). This was in the early days. He was covered with puss filled sores and his clothes stuck to his body because of this. His eyes were swollen to the point that they were just slits. The smell that accompanied him was disgusting to everyone except Amma. He waited outside the doorway watching until Amma had finished hugging. At this point, Amma motioned to him to come in. She began biting and sucking the puss and blood from his wounds. The scene was so repulsive that some vomited and others fainted. Yet Amma continued undaunted and performed this healing ritual on him a number of times until he was cured. It is miraculous that she cured the leper and it is also miraculous that she did not contract the disease herself after sucking so much puss and blood from his sores. There are video clips of this scene in a DVD titled *Vintage Scenes* and also on YouTube® by searching "Amma Cures Dattan the Leper."

Amma with Dattan the Leper

Raising People from the Dead

There are two instances of this in the biography. In one of them, a young girl with asthma died of an attack at the hospital. Pronounced dead by the doctors, the grandmother took the girl to Amma's temple and laid her on Amma's seat wailing with grief all the time. Amma, who was at a nearby house doing a puja ceremony, suddenly became very restless and left immediately for the temple. When she got there, she put the girl's body on her lap and meditated until the girl started to move and come back to life. In another instance a girl who was fated to die by poisonous snake bite was bitten, died and then brought back to life by Amma.

Predicting the Future

There are numerous instances described in the back of the biography in which Amma warned individuals about pending calamities then gave them a formula to overcome it. For example, she warned one family of a pending death which could be transferred to a domestic animal if the formula were observed. In this case, the family dog got into a fight with a cobra and both died as a result. The family member was spared.

Dispensing Divine Births

There are a number of instances described in the biography in which a couple that was unable to conceive, were gifted a child by Amma. In one of these episodes, the woman was hugely pregnant after 16 months and doctors could still not see any baby – only a smoky mass. At a certain point Amma told them to go to the hospital and a healthy baby was born by caesarian section. Amma says about these events that she goes into meditation and a power is transferred from her to the childless woman.

Going Without Sleep

Amma normally sleeps about an hour a day. Even then she is aware of everything that is going on about her. This is called the Fourth State or Turiya. The three normal states are waking, dreaming and deep sleep. When one attains Turiya, consciousness remains unbroken through all the other three states. One of Amma's senior swamis once told the author he had seen her go seven days without any sleep. It is common for her to go several days with no sleep.

This is a short review of a few instances in which Amma used her divine powers for the uplifting of devotees. More can be explored by reading Amma's biography and the *Awaken Children* books.

A Blazing Sun of Compassion

Reading Amma's biography written by Swami Amritaswarupananda, we get a glimpse of Amma's intensely compassionate nature which began as a small girl and continues unabated to this day.

We have already mentioned hugging millions of people and how Amma is motivated to do this because of her immense love and compassion.

We have visited her near daily exits from this world in her early years about which she commented that she had to make an effort to stay in this world and this was done out of her compassion for suffering humanity. She instructed those close to her to chant certain mantras and sing certain songs to coax her back because there was a danger of her not returning.

Jesus said that we could know a true prophet by their fruit. No saint in the history of the world has produced as much fruit in the span of their lifetimes as Amma. And Amma is not done yet!

Amma's Charities

> "Thus, by their fruit you will recognize them." Jesus, *Matthew* 7:20, NIV

It is mind numbing to consider all of Amma's charities. It is doubly astonishing to consider that all this has been put in place by a woman with only a fourth-grade education. This inspiring story of love and compassion is described in detail in Amma's biography.

Amma's charities are run by Amma's disciples and volunteers. There are no paid executives making wages or salaries.

It should be noted that Amma herself lives a life of great austerity occupying a very small space of only a few hundred square feet at her ashram. She wears only the plainest white clothes and has virtually no personal possessions other than a few items like an ink pen and a hairbrush. When she is flying, she insists on riding in the economy seats.

There is a wonderful documentary about Amma's numerous charities titled *Embracing the World*. At the time of this writing, it is available for free on YouTube and it is highly recommended to watch it to get the full scope and impact of Amma's charities.

Helping Women

Vocational Training for 100,000 Women

To equip economically vulnerable women with the skills and means to set up cottage industries, more than 6,000 self-help groups for women across India and 1,000 groups in the nearby Andaman Islands have been established.

Microcredit Loans Get Them Started

So far, ETW has helped 3,500 of these groups receive microcredit loans -- benefitting more than 60,000 families.

Life & Accident Insurance to Protect their Family's Future

Every member of the self-help groups has been enrolled in a plan with the Life Insurance Corporation of India. As part of the agreement, the insurance company also provides scholarships to 15% of the policyholder's children. Each year, these scholarships will rotate, so every family can benefit.

Training for 100,000 Home Nurses

Education

Main campus of Amrita University

- 100,000 scholarships for children from desperately impoverished agricultural communities and those affected by AIDS
- Special schools for the hearing-impaired and mentally challenged
- Award winning literacy and vocational training for adults from India's poorest tribal communities, offering over 100 courses ranging from candle making to computer science
- Free vocational training for 500 teenagers in 11 trades with an 80% graduation rate
- A secondary school with 3,500 students, the largest school in the Indian State of Kerala

Disaster Relief

A mobile telemedicine unit the size of a large bus takes sophisticated medical service to disaster-stricken areas.

$1 Million: Earthquake and Tsunami in Japan, 2011

- $10.7 million: Karnataka / Andhra Pradesh Floods, 2009
- Food, clothing, bedding and blankets distributed
- Medical care for 500+ people per day

$465,000: Bihar Floods, 2008

- Medical team in place for two months, treating 50,000
- Thousands of tents, blankets and tarpaulins distributed

$1 Million: Hurricane Katrina, 2005

$46 Million: Indian Ocean Tsunami, 2004

Building Homes

- Building not just 100,000 homes for the homeless but whole communities complete with town halls, roads, wells, electricity, sewage systems and clean drinking water
- More than 1,600 families relocated from slums into new apartments
- 6,200 new homes for victims of the Indian Ocean Tsunami
- 2,000 new homes for flood victims in Raichur
- 1,200 new homes for victims of the Gujarat Earthquake in 2009

Care Homes for Children

Kerala, India

Running an orphanage for 500 children for the last 20 years, where the children consistently win awards in music, sports and dance. More than 1 in 3 go on to earn college degrees

Kenya, Africa

In April 2011, during Amma's visit to Nairobi, the Vice-President of the Republic of Kenya opened the Amrita Watoto Boma Care Home for Children. Initially, the children's home will accommodate 50 children.

Two other projects were also inaugurated:

- A Vocational Training Centre, equipped with 35 computers to serve the nearby slum settlement, and
- A Drinking Water Distribution Project will provide daily, clean drinking water

Fighting Hunger

- Feeding more than 10 million people a year in India
- Distributing uncooked rice, milk and other staples to deeply impoverished communities
- Providing six million free meals and 185 tons of uncooked rice in the first six months after the 2006 Indian Ocean Tsunami
- Serving more than 100,000 meals every year to the homeless and hungry internationally
- Feeding more than 75,000 people every year in 40 cities throughout North America

Healthcare

- More than $60 Million in free medical care since 1998
- 5.5 Million patients treated - 2 Million patients treated for free
- AIMS Hospitals: 1,450 beds with an attached medical college with a 400 bed facility, offering free or subsidized care

AIMS Hospital in Kochi, Kerala, India

As of this writing construction has started on a 2,000 bed hospital in Delhi.

- A Mobile Telemedicine Unit, the size of a city bus, bringing sophisticated medical care to remote areas
- More than 100 free medical drives in remote, impoverished areas. When necessary, patients go to the hospital for free.
- 25 bed hospital near a remote hilltop temple provides for the hundreds of thousands who make the pilgrimage every year
- Medical dispensary in Mumbai

- HIV/AIDS care center, open daily, providing anti-retroviral drugs and care services
- Free cataract surgeries: 726 patients in 2010
- Pain and Palliative Home Care: 75,000 impoverished, terminally ill patients treated annually -- all free of charge

Monthly Pensions for 50,000 Widows, the Disabled & Victims of Poverty

Recognizing that due to a loss or injury, people in the developing world can easily be consigned to a lifetime of hardship, these pensions don't expire - they are for life. Ultimately, 100,000 men, women and children will receive monthly pensions.

Care homes for the Elderly

They come for refuge or to spend their final years in a tranquil spiritual ambiance. These four care homes also hold community functions & cultural programs.

Sponsored Weddings for the Poor

In India, marriage is essential for the stability of the entire family. For decades, Amma has sponsored weddings, providing all the items necessary for a traditional service.

Hospital Visits and Meals on Wheels

Volunteers throughout the works visit hospitals, nursing homes and the elderly and in firm in their own homes.

Green Initiatives

- In Kerala, India, three medicinal plant gardens conserve coastal, midland and forest ecosystems and provide employment for local women.
- In France, Amma's volunteers built a walk-in bee sanctuary that offers the educational experience of living with bees.
- In Europe, Greenfriends is using organic cultivation methods and developing seed banks to preserve local, ancient and/or endangered seeds.
- In the USA, Embracing the World has launched a tree sponsorship program with

the goal of reforesting 80 acres of land with 40,000 pine trees.

- In India, volunteers are using non-recyclable hard plastic packing straps to weave bed bases for metal-framed foldaway beds for disaster survivors.
- Amma Fiji's Green Friends picked up hundreds of plastic bags and bottles, pieces of foam, and even some tires. Around 60 bags of garbage was picked up on two beaches along the Suva Sea Wall.
- Green Shores project is planning on planting 300,000 casuarina saplings in total on the Alappad Panchayat peninsula.

Public Health

The Amala Bharatam Campaign has the potential to have a powerful impact on India's public health goals. Lack of sanitation is the world's leading cause of infection. It aims to improve public health and restore India's physical beauty. By cleaning India's public spaces, promoting health through hygiene, sorting garbage, recycling, and properly disposing of waste, awareness of this campaign has reached millions.

More than 1,000 clean-up drives have been undertaken on the fourth Sunday of each month, which has been designated as Clean Sunday. Through ABC, volunteers are cleaning public areas, constructing public toilets and spreading awareness in schools regarding the proper way to dispose of trash. Handkerchiefs have been distributed to more than one million school children. Teaching them to use them instead of spitting on the ground.

Research for a Better World

- Researchers at Amrita University deployed the world's first wireless sensor network system for landslide detection in Munnar, Kerala. Warning of an impending landslide, it allows for early evacuation and disaster management.

- SAVE program has developed educational applications using multimedia, virtual reality and haptic technologies to simulate real-life situations and provide portable, cost-effective, scalable and vocational education.

- MoVE (Mobile Vocational Education), utilizes vehicles powered by solar energy to provide vocational education for sustainable development in diverse areas, including India's remote tribal communities.
- Amma's Center for Nanosciences is conducting research into cancer, infectious diseases and tissue engineering.
- In 2011, A-VIEW (Amrita Virtual Interactive E-learning World) won the Jury Award for *Best Innovation in Open and Distance Learning* at the World Education Summit in New Delhi.
- Over 27,000 students in rural schools are using the India's first computer-aided adaptive assessment and learning program CREATE (Centre for Research in Advanced Technologies for Education).

Amma and Jesus

First off, your author would like to state plainly and clearly that he has a deep personal love for Jesus and there is a feeling of knowing him personally. This has resulted in writing two books about the Master

It is also your author's opinion that the second coming of Jesus is Amma, a.k.a. Mata Amritanandamayi. We will not find anyone in history who has lived the life that Jesus taught as completely and as powerfully and as voluminously as Amma. But this is just the opinion of one voice crying in the wilderness. Amma would not consider this discussion to be of any importance.

Jesus had two commandments for us – love your God with all your heart, mind, strength and soul and love your neighbor as yourself. This is also the path Amma recommends. Learn to cry tears for God.

"If you can pray to Him [Her] with an open heart and shed a few tears out of love for Him, then you are saved." Amma, *Eternal Wisdom*, vol. II

Amma emphasizes serving the poor, the sick and the elderly just as Jesus did. Serve others and relieve suffering in the world.

Love is the core of the life and teaching of Jesus and Amma also says her religion is love.

Some may feel that the crucifixion of Jesus sets him apart from all others. Amma is crucified each time she sits hugging for 12 or 14 hours which is more than half of the days in a year. The pain her body endures day in and day out is tremendous. According to the Bible, Jesus was crucified for 6 hours before he was taken down from the cross. Amma has been crucified for 40 years. Amma also died and was "raised from the dead" 8 hours later as recounted in the chapter *Supernormal Powers*.

Swamini Krishnamrita devotes Chapter 6 titled *Fresh as a Daisy* in her book *Love is the Answer* to explain the intense physical pain and hardship Amma endures and has endured for many years. This is to help us understand the phenomenal sacrifice Amma makes for our benefit. Here is an excerpt:

"Sometimes I think about how much pain Amma has in Her body from giving darshan for such extremely long hours. On some occasions She can barely bend Her neck or move Her body at all without it hurting. At times like these I wonder how She will be able to embrace five people let alone a program full of 20,000 people! Amma never thinks in this way. She knows that She has the capacity to detach Herself from the mind/body connection; She is always able to find the strength to do anything that needs to be done to serve others. *Swamini Krishnamrita*

Amma comments on the weight she carries which is the pain she experiences:

"Sundays are the most crowded days and many devotees had come. The Holy Mother received one and all. The cough troubled Her several times, and the devotees were greatly pained at heart. A young man who was very devoted said, "Mother, it is unbearable to see you suffering. Give some of it to me."

"Mother: (laughingly) This love is good, but son, you know, it would be impossible for others to bear even an infinitesimal fraction of this weight." *Amma, Awaken Children, vol. 1*

Occasionally, dogged persistence by a questioner will solicit an admission of divinity. The following is a quote from the fourth quarter 1997 *Amirtanandam* magazine in which a 12-year-old named Sarada interviews Amma.

Sarada: Are you and Jesus the same?

Amma: (laughs)

Sarada: Did it hurt to be nailed to the cross?

Amma: It was his will. Jesus was the guru. Whatever happens to the guru is his will. Jesus did not need to suffer on the cross, but he did it to show the world the meaning of sacrifice. It is also symbolic of the death of the ego while still in the body.

Sarada: Are you and Jesus the same?

Amma: You could say that Amma is one with the consciousness of Christ; the important thing is to find that in yourself. The same consciousness that was in Jesus is in Amma now. Amma has come for the same reason as

Jesus. God is Pure Consciousness, Jesus is the guru.

Sarada: Is your soul Jesus' soul?

Amma: Yes! (emphatically looking at Sarada)

Sarada: How can I be like that?

Amma: Look inside there (pointing to Sarada's heart). Don't worry about the past or the future.

One could say the Divine Mother or Christ that embodied as Jesus, returned as Amma but amplified by many magnitudes.

In the history of the human race, no one has done so much for so many in such a short amount of time as Amma.

Amma and Ramakrishna

It was mentioned earlier in this book that Sri Ramakrishna (1836-1886) displayed some of the same divine qualities as Amma such as granting spiritual transmissions (divine experiences) and going spontaneously into ecstatic states of love for the Divine. However, Amma has been a much more powerful, far reaching and voluminous manifestation than Ramakrishna.

There appears to be some association between the incarnation of Amma and the incarnation of Ramakrishna. Your author will present the information here and the reader can make of it what they will.

Amma and Ramakrishna both worshipped the Divine Mother and specifically the form of Kali (destroyer of the ego).

In the early years (and the practice may persist to this day) new arrivals at Amma's ashram were given a copy of the *Gospel of Ramakrishna* to read as an introduction to spirituality. Later, when the first full size temple was built on ashram grounds

– the Kali Temple – there was only one major statue of a deity installed and that is Mother Kali.

Amma requested that the statue be made in an exact likeness of the Kali statue in Dakshineswar that Ramakrishna worshiped and that the statue be made by the same family that made the original Dakshineswar statue around 1856.

After some years of having renunciates live in her ashram, Amma instituted the practice of initiating those who had come to live with her into *sanyasa* (renunciates). Starting out first as brahmacharins and brahmacharinis (male and female), these renunciates would eventually graduate to be a swami or swamini at which time they would wear orange clothing which symbolizes the destruction of the ego in the fire of Truth.

Amma, adhering to tradition, did not initiate them. The first to become a swami was Balu who is now Swami Amritaswarupananda and the writer of Amma's biography and the *Awaken Children* dialogue books. He was initiated into the Ramakrishna Order of monks by a swami in that order. Then in turn, Swami Amritaswarupananda, initiated all those who followed him. All of them in the Ramakrishna Order.

At a point later in time, Amma stopped the process of initiating people for a reason that is known only to Amma.

Ramakrishna stated that his incarnation was a "scouting mission" and that he would return to this world in approximately 100 years. At that time, he said he would grant liberation to many people and those that did not take advantage of the opportunity at that time would have to wait a very long time for another opportunity to present itself.

Ramakrishna passed away in 1886 and Amma was born in 1953 which was 67 years. It was not quite a hundred but Ramakrishna's use of a rounded number (100) indicates he could have been approximating. Had he said 97 years we could more easily take that to be an exact number.

Liberation or *mukti* means to get off the wheel of birth and death known as *samsara*. The cycling of birth and death is caused by a state of ignorance in the mind whereby it wrongly perceives that it is separate from everyone and everything with this being supported by the illusory feeling of "I" and "mine." The nature of samsara is suffering. Therefore, it is most desirable to transcend this condition which can be rightly viewed as a wretched state of being. Samsara is thoroughly discussed in both Buddhist and Hindu spiritual texts. To do this, one requires the help of a Self-realized being and these beings are very rare.

Amma says this:

> "To be born as a human is very rare... It is rarer still to have an interest in Liberation... And extremely rare to have a relationship with God in the form of the Guru.... If we waste our life even after gaining these three, it is like a pitch-dark night..."

As discussed earlier in this book, Amma is the Jubilee Amma whereby her incredible spiritual power can grant liberation to many people. She has said that most persons who faithfully chant the mantra she has given them will be given liberation at the end of their life. Those for whom liberation just cannot yet be given will be granted an exceptional birth which affords every opportunity to make great progress toward liberation.

Over time, your author has read most all books about Ramakrishna and years ago, came across the quote in which Ramakrishna stated that he would return in a hundred years to grant liberation to spiritual seekers. Your author has not since been able to find the quote so you will have to take my word for it. The quote was also mentioned in a 2017 Matruvani magazine (Amma's organization publishes this) in a story told by devotees who had also been devotees of Ramakrishna.

Russell Brand and Amma

Amma and Yogananda

Sri Paramahansa Yogananda (1893-1952) was also very much like Amma in that he put much emphasis on love and devotion as a path and worshipped the Divine Mother - specifically the form of Kali.

A long time Yogananda devotee, Anand, went to see Amma in 1997. He then visited her at her ashram in Amritapuri. The following is from the July, 2017 *Matruvani* magazine:

> "Every time Amma visited Spain, I would attend Her programs. In 2000, I felt like going to Amritapuri. I did. There, I asked Amma if She was my Guru. She said, "Yes." I also asked Her about Yogananda and the lineage of Gurus from which He had descended. Amma said, "I am Yogananda." Amma dissolved all my doubts while I stayed in the ashram, where I lived until 2008."

Yogananda passed away in 1952 and Amma was born in 1953.

One way to interpret these associations with Ramakrishna and Yogananda is to see these as incarnations of one Divine Mother who pulled out all of the stops to save mankind when she embodied as Amma. In Amma the Divine Mother has manifested an unprecedented amount of spiritual power to fulfill this mission.

Jane Goodall and Amma

Amma with Pope Francis

Amma with Narendra Modi the current Prime Minister of India

He consults with her and gives talks at her birthday celebrations.

Amma's Main Ashram – Amritapuri

The Main Hall at Amritapuri

Amma at Trivandrum 2007

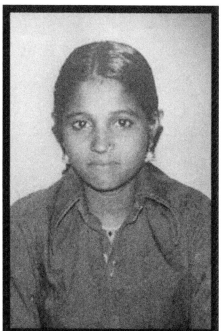

At this age
Amma had
merged with
the Divine
Mother and
was in
possession of
all yogic
powers.

Amma: "The purpose of our human birth is to realize our own true nature."

Wisdom is knowing we are all one.

Love is what it feels like

And Compassion is what it acts like.

Dear Reader – If you enjoyed this book please consider posting a review on Amazon. If you did not enjoy it then email me instead – lol!

Love and peace to you always!

Other Books by the Author

Read about or purchase any of Ethan's other books:

www.devipress.com or on Amazon® do a search for Ethan Walker III

AMMA IS LOVE

Exploring Amma's Theory and Practice of Love as a Way of Life

Love is mysterious! On one hand, it is the only thing that can save us from perpetual darkness; the world from chaos and disintegration. On the other hand, very few of us feel any love day in and day out for our entire lifetimes. Love is self-luminous bliss; it is light; it is life. It is the core of our being and yet it has been lost and forgotten to the world because it means the death of our egos. There is a subconscious revulsion to love. It is grossly misunderstood, universally dismissed and relegated to a back-room shelf in the warehouse of humanity. For most, it is simply a four-letter word.

Amma (Mata Amritanandamayi) not only understands love but she is the most brilliant manifestation of love the world has ever seen. She says her religion is love; she is love incarnate. Yet few of us have any knowledge as to how we might practice love. There is no understanding as to what it means to grow and cultivate love in our own hearts on a day by day basis.

Love is the only Truth that makes life meaningful. Life without love is death. This book is an exploration of Amma's voluminous teachings on how to practice love. The cultivation of love requires much effort because the ego will oppose it at every turn. This is because God is love and love means the end of our egos. Each day we can practice love – love for the Divine, love for all the beings in the universe and the universe as a whole. We can feel love - deeply - with our whole being! This is the simplest, most effective and most powerful path to eternal bliss. - To review further or purchase, go to www.devipress.com or search for Ethan Walker III on Amazon®.

CONVERSATIONS WITH THE DIVINE MOTHER OF THE UNIVERSE

Conversations is a candid discussion with the Divine Mother of the Universe. The author, Ethan Walker, asks her about the meaning of life, the mysteries of existence, what to do about suffering, who or what we are, the way to happiness, how to be a whole and complete person, how to successfully navigate life and much more. The Divine Mother reveals her nature, her perspectives and her love in a way that fills our hearts with bliss and peace. The Divine Mother is a beacon of hope in a world gone mad. She is personable, accessible and clear in her revelations of the deepest secrets and mysteries of life.   This is a book that you will want to read many times because it is blissful, divinely intoxicating and it shows us the way forward. The Divine Mother's innocence, love and compassion floats like a fragrant, gossamer, shining cloud just on top of this bubbling brew of inspired words.

THE ECSTATIC BLISS
OF BEING

This book is an invitation to experience the ecstatic bliss of being. It can be likened to planting and growing a garden of tremendous joy in the soil of one's own mind and heart. There is nothing more deeply satisfying or inspiring than to watch and feel the colorful blooms of cosmic insight growing from our deepest Self.

Through the doors of this book are snippets and tweaks of ruddy truth and sparkling gems of vibrant love and mountains of profound aliveness. All of it provided as an exciting adventure into the timeless reality of Being.

Written by Ethan Walker the author of over twenty books on spirituality. This is a marvelous collection of short adventures into the bliss of the transcendent and the immanent – the Ancient of Days that percolates from the core of being in every person's heart.

INTO THE MYSTIC

A Story of Light, Love and Bodacious Spiritual Adventures

In 1967 at the age of nineteen, Ethan was unsuspectingly catapulted from his self-imposed, fortress of atheism to swimming in the ocean of the Divine in one blinding, mind-melting flash of insight. He never

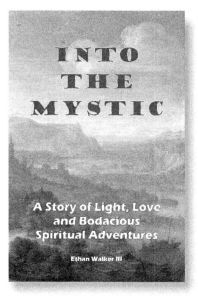

looked back. This is the story of a lifetime of spiritual pursuit. From hippies and the cultural revolution to the Rosicrucians to the I Am School to the Summit Lighthouse to Self-inquiry (non-duality) to love and devotion – bhakti - with priceless guidance from his guru Amma beginning in 1988. This is one man's journey, spanning more than fifty years, through the brambles and the thickets; through the ancient halls of mystery, the pure emptiness of being and into the bliss of the Divine Light. This is a story of love, love and more love; a transfiguration from mind to Heart. To review or purchase go to www.devipress.com or search for Ethan Walker III on Amazon.

HOW TO BE REALLY HAPPY!

The Path to Deep Happiness

Would you like to be happy all the time – overflowing with joy? Bliss? Love? If your answer is "Yes," then you will want to read this book. Happiness waits in the oasis of our hearts calling us day after day to come home. We only need to know where  to look and how to go there because, as it turns out, we have been looking in all the wrong places. This search for happiness is something every human being has in common. From the day we are born, we begin to look for happiness. Every action we perform is for this purpose yet we remain discontent to the day we die. Most of us fail to see the simple truth. Not understanding that love, bliss and joy are already within us, as our own eternal nature, we never chart a course for this most important of all adventures. And the best part is our inner happiness doesn't care what we have done or not done in the past – saint and sinner alike are equally welcome.

This book is an opportunity - a road map - to discover the sublime, ecstatic, joyous, blissful, love-soaked reality of our own infinite being. This is true happiness and it is not dependent on anything outside of ourselves. It is self-luminous and undeniable and it waits for our return at the center of the Heart. In fact, simply reading this book will make you feel happy!

To review further or purchase, go to www.devipress.com or search for Ethan Walker III on Amazon®.

BIG LOVE
AND SPIRITUAL BLISS

Every spiritual path, every endeavor to understand, every word ever spoken leads to Love. Every moment of joy and every drop of suffering lead to Love. Every desire and every fear; every pleasure and pain – all of it leads to Love. Love is the very pinnacle of human existence – there is nothing higher nor nothing deeper. It is the subtlest of the subtle, beyond reckoning – formless and unchanging – yet it gives meaning to the endless dance of existence.

This Love is the thread upon which the bead of every soul is strung and it is the fire in every star. It is the light of non-duality manifesting in the realm of the many. It is at the core of every heart whether human, plant, animal or mineral.

We have been wandering in the dark catacombs of our minds for far too long – separated from the Cosmic Mind - our Beloved - and so we find ourselves endlessly plying the oceans of our burning discontent in our ships of vacant dreams. This book is a knock on our door where life waits to take us in its arms; where Love simmers in the cauldron of our remembering.

Our very being is that Love which frolics as an innocent child and it has come for us at last. In this book is a map to endless bliss.

To review further or purchase, go to www.devipress.com or search for Ethan Walker III on Amazon®.

THE UPANISHADS

In the Light of the Divine Mother

The Upanishads have been a door to the Divine Mysteries for thousands of years. It has been studied by mystics, yogis, philosophers and physicists. "In the whole world there is no study so beneficial and so elevating as that of the Upanishads. It  has been the solace of my life. It will be the solace of my death." - Arthur Schopenhauer (1788-1860) German philosopher. "I go to the Upanishads to ask questions." - Neils Bohr (1885-1962) – Nobel Prize winning Danish physicist.

This version of the Upanishads has been adapted and rewritten by Ethan Walker III to clarify and simplify the truth contained therein. There is also the addition of the Divine Mother of the Universe as the creatrix and the actor on the stage of awareness. Brahman is awareness – changeless, motionless and empty yet that which grants aliveness to all things.

The Divine Mother is all that is form – eternally changing form. She is the cosmic mind that directs all things. Brahman, as pure, primordial awareness, is that which is eternally changeless. The Divine Mother is that which is eternally changing. Together, Brahman and the Divine Mother are not-two.

To review further or purchase, go to www.devipress.com or search for Ethan Walker III on Amazon®.

THE LIGHT OF
PRIMORDIAL AWARENESS

This is a guide to the realization of one's own Self. It is closer than the air we breathe. It is hidden in plain sight. It is the Philosopher's Stone that transforms the mind into the molten gold of light and love. There is no undertaking that is more important as it is the bridge to liberation.

Written in plain, simple, easy to grasp terms, *The Primordial Light of Awareness* is a down to earth revelation of this Ancient Truth. Step by step each point of contemplation untangles our mental and emotional blindness and leads the mind to the blissful ocean of awareness. All that is not our Self is stripped away.

Step by step we begin to feel the lightness of our original innocence and our hearts begin to open letting in the light of love and joy.

To review further or purchase, go to www.devipress.com or search for Ethan Walker III on Amazon®.

DEATH OF THE EGO

The Path to Endless Bliss!

The ego is the cause of all our mental and emotional suffering as well as all the strife and wars in the world. By *ego* we mean the fundamental thought of an "I." This I-thought has taken up residence in our minds and it is not our true self – it is an imposter. It is the feeling of separation from God, Nature and others. It is the sense of "I" and "mine." Thus, it is our egoistic minds that obscure the truth of our existence which is this: we are all beings if infinite bliss, love and joy! Happiness is our primal nature! There can be no Self-realization, God-realization, merging in the Divine, coming to Jesus or dissolving into the ocean of nirvana without abandoning that great thief and liar the ego. Most of us imagine our egos to be our friend but it is really our greatest enemy.

This book explores the nature of the ego, its origins and how we might at last rid ourselves of this torment. Most of us will not be rid of the great liar immediately but every effort to move in that direction will remove some of our suffering. Even a little reduction in the illusions and delusions of our egos will give us great benefit and a deeper more satisfying peace, love and joy.

The spiritual path is not about getting, acquiring or gaining anything. It is 100% about removing something and that something is the ego. Once removed, the truth of our magnificent luminous being is revealed. We will realize the ego had been no more than a phantom – an illusion – and we are free, liberated, saved and eternally reunited with the Divine. We are free to swim in the ocean of bliss!

To review further or purchase, go to www.devipress.com or search for Ethan Walker III on Amazon®.

SPIRITUALITY IS SOMETHING WE FEEL

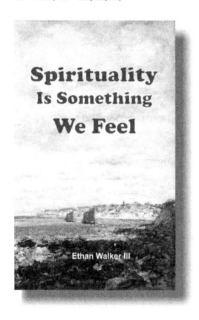

Peace, joy, bliss, love, compassion - these are some of the ways we feel our spiritual nature. The mind ever attempts to grapple with the realm of the spiritual but the spiritual will never fit inside the small box we call the mind. Only the heart can know the light and love that reside at the core of each and every being.

This book is an exploration of ways in which we can feel the Divine. All words, beliefs and concepts fall away in the presence of direct spiritual experience. At best these can only serve as a map to the door of endless bliss. That door is none other than our own heart.

THE MYSTIC CHRIST

The Light of Non-duality and the Path of Love According to the Life and Teachings of Jesus

The Mystic Christ is an ancient tale of mystic union, salvation, and enlightenment. It is the careful uncovering of a lost treasure of immeasurable value, long buried in the suffocating darkness of conventional

orthodoxy on one side, and blind fundamentalist extremism on the other. From the viewpoint of the world's mystical religious traditions, the brilliant light of the Master's way is revealed as a penetrating radical non-duality unifying all people and all of life. His path to this all-embracing unity is the spiritual practice of pure selfless love. Love God intensely, love our neighbor as our own Self, bless those that curse us, and pray for those that mistreat us. Love has been lost, becoming nothing more than a word in the dictionary and, yet, it remains the foundation of Jesus' message.

The Mystic Christ is also a compelling story of the ego, the personification of ignorance, and how it has distorted and subverted the sublime sayings of the Master, twisting reality into unreality and light into darkness. The ego is the Antichrist in this ancient drama that has gripped every culture for all time in its talons of self-centered perception. The ego is anti-love.

Adam and Eve were not the first people, the nature of man is good, scripture is not infallible, Jesus is one of the ways, all religions are paths to

God, reincarnation is in the Bible, the resurrection as a personal spiritual awakening, and the error of eternal damnation are all carefully and lovingly revealed in the life and sayings of Jesus.

The Mystic Christ is thoroughly punctuated with quotes from Buddha, Krishna, Lao Tzu and other masters of the mystical traditions. But, most importantly, over 230 scriptural references from the Old and New Testament are used to illustrate the harmony that exists between the life and teachings of Jesus and the world's great religions.

The author removes 2000 years of ego-centered bindings that have hidden the brilliant light of the Master from the world. *The Mystic Christ* is at once profoundly fascinating, deeply historic and electric with the vibration of the mystical experience. To review further or purchase, go to www.devipress.com or search for Ethan Walker III on Amazon®.

FINDING GOD'S LOVE

The Theory and Practice of Love and Devotion as a Spiritual Path

\Love is the primal essence. Love is the light of the Divine which fills the vastness of eternity with the sweet fragrance of immortal bliss. The practice of love and devotion is an ancient path leading to direct mystical experience of the Supreme. Notable teachers of this path include Jesus, Hafiz, Narada, Ramprasad, and Amma (Mata Amritanandamayi). *Finding God's Love* is suitable for any pilgrim of any faith who wishes to experience a direct and personal communion with the Divine. God's lovers will find immediate access to the living room of God's heart where they will revel in the bliss and joy of the universe;

divinely intoxicated in the breath of the eternally radiant now; swept away in an endless celebration of life.

The first part of the book reveals how love works to release the human psyche from the fetters of its own self-imposed limitations. Love is the antidote to all negative emotions. Love heals the festering wounds that lay buried in our past. Love cleans the lens of the soul allowing the light of the Divine to percolate up from the center of our being illuminating our personal world. The second part of the book explains the practical aspects of this path including meditations, visualizations and prayer. The last section is a collection of teachings from Amma, the hugging saint, on the practice of love and devotion.

Love is what makes life beautiful because God *is* love. Love nourishes the delicate flowering of the immortal soul vanquishing boredom once and for all in the magnificence of its ever-fresh ever-mysterious river of divine grace. This book is an invitation to ecstasy - to swim in the ocean of God. To review further or purchase, go to www.devipress.com or search for Ethan Walker III on Amazon®.

BHAKTI SUTRAS OF NARADA

The Spiritual Path of Endless Love

These Bhakti Sutras were written by Narada who is a sage of cosmic dimensions and who appears throughout classic Hindu spiritual literature going back thousands of years. These sutras are a collection of 84 phrases or aphorisms designed to lead one up the mountain path of spiritual devotion. Each is like a flower strung on a common thread. Bhakti - love for the Beloved - is the highest pinnacle of any spiritual endeavor. It is a wholly selfless path in which the practitioner is unconcerned with personal gain or spiritual goals. The aim is simply to love God. In this path one experiences the bliss of the Divine from the very outset. As Ramakrishna says, God's devotees are invited into the living room of God's heart from the very beginning while others must wait outside until the very end. Bhakti is the simplest, safest, easiest, most satisfying and most blissful path to the Divine. Commentary and parallel quotes from other Masters have been provided by the author. Come walk in God's spiritual garden and smell the roses of Divine Love!

To review further or purchase, go to www.devipress.com or search for Ethan Walker III on Amazon®.

108 Hugs for Jesus

The Ecstasy of Divine Love as a Path to God

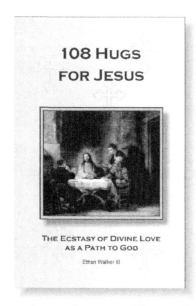

What every soul longs for is to experience the Divine directly, personally and intimately. To have this direct communion is the purpose of our human birth and nothing else in all of eternity will ever satisfy us or truly make us happy. The path to this is hidden and few tread it. It is not something that can be found in any church or any book as it must be searched for and discovered in the Heart. At the center of our being, enshrined in the Sacred Heart that sits in our own chest is a portal to God's infinite light, love and bliss. It is here, within us, that God waits for us – calling for us – yearning for our love. Jesus said in *Luke 17:21* that the kingdom of

God is within us. This book is a guide to this fulfilling pursuit - the Divine Romance; the lover and the Beloved; the eternal Companion.

Jesus prescribed a path to this ecstatic union with His two commandments – love your God with all your heart, mind, soul and strength and love your neighbor as your own self. He called them commandments and said there are no commandments greater than these. In Luke 10:25, Jesus says practicing these two commandments is all that is necessary to attain eternal life.

In this book is a collection of 108 phrases describing key aspects of the Lord's teachings and life events. By chanting these with love and devotion, we can, day by day, increase the fire of our love for the Lord.

Also in this book, is a thorough discussion of the practice of Jesus' commandments including techniques and pitfalls. Love is what every soul needs more than anything else. Love is what is most needed in the world. Orthodox beliefs such as Jesus being the only way, Jesus dying to wash away our sins, the nature of sin and reincarnation are discussed. - To review further or purchase, go

to www.devipress.com or search for Ethan
Walker III on Amazon®.

WHOLE FOODS
PLANT BASED DIET

**Save the Earth, Save your Health, Save the
Animals**

Feel good, regain
your health, lose
weight effortlessly
and throw away the
medicine bottles.
This is the single
most effective path
one can take to
restore health and
vitality. But there is
more to this than
just good health.
Animal agriculture
is also destroying
our planet, and causing intense suffering for

billions of farmed animals. 90 percent of the clearing of the rainforest in South America is for the raising of beef cattle. Farmed animals produce more greenhouse gas than all modes of human transportation combined.

The practice is very wasteful and inefficient as it takes eleven pounds of grain to make one pound of beef. Animal agriculture consumes more fresh water by far than all human consumption combined. And this is only the tip of the iceberg.

According to the United Nations and the World Health Organization, we will need to stop the practice of animal agriculture if the human race is to survive. The seriousness of this cannot be understated. The practice of raising livestock for human consumption is wholly unsustainable.

Most people are not aware of the horrific suffering animals endure at the hands of profit motivated meat and dairy producing enterprises. Animals endure this suffering and have been enslaved by human kind for only one reason and that is to satisfy our taste buds. This is the worst of all possible reasons to ask an animal to suffer and to slaughtered at a very young age.

Numerous comprehensive scientific studies such as the China Study, have proven beyond all doubt that eating animal flesh and dairy products is very detrimental to our health causing, cancer, heart attacks, strokes, diabetes and many more debilitating diseases.

Read this booklet and watch the videos *Forks Over Knives, Cowspiracy* and *Earthlings*. Do some research and then change to a plant-based, whole-foods cuisine. Save the earth, save your health and save the animals! Do it now before it's too late!

To review further or purchase, go to www.devipress.com or search for Ethan Walker III on Amazon®.

A Pilgrim's Guide to Amma

A Field Handbook for Entering and Exploring
the World of Mata Amritanandamayi

Mata
Amritanandamayi,
commonly known
as Amma, is a
mysterious and
supremely
powerful river of
unconditional love.
Having never taken
even a single breath
for herself, she has
come to this world
only to give. The

**A PILGRIM'S GUIDE
TO AMMA**

A FIELD HANDBOOK
FOR EXPLORING THE DIVINE WORLD
OF MATA AMRITANANDAMAYI

Ethan Walker III

rest of us, as seekers, as children of light, have a
very rare opportunity in being able to have access
to such a Divine phenomenon. If we are suffering
she gives comfort. If we are intent on the Divine,
she gives instruction and direct experience. She
is always giving with a tremendous outpouring

of love and compassion that is a wonder to behold.

Amma asks nothing in return. We can keep our religion or current path if we like. We are not asked to sign up for anything. Amma will help is with whatever spiritual endeavor we may have undertaken – no strings attached. Amma says her religion is love.

Amma's "largeness" is beyond understanding but what we can see is profoundly astonishing. It is the purpose of this book to give a brief view of Amma's life, accomplishments and her uplifting impact on people just like us. We will have to look far and wide in the scrolls of human history to find a Divine manifestation that has done as much for humanity, is as powerful as Amma and, at the same time, so supremely accessible to anyone and everyone.

In the past 40 years Amma has tirelessly hugged over 34 million people. Why would anyone do this and do it for free? This alone speaks to the fact that Amma is a Divine person extraordinarily endowed with the ocean of Divine Shakti (power) and limitless love. Her charities for the poor and the suffering are vast. It boggles the mind to consider that all this was done by a short, cute Indian lady, born into a very poor family who never made it past the fourth grade. Dear reader, you are invited to step into this book and see what Amma has to offer you.

To review further or purchase, go to www.devipress.com or search for Ethan Walker III on Amazon®.

RAMA'S MOST EXCELLENT DISPASSION

The Path to Bliss

Over 5,000 years ago, Rama, the God Man / avatar, walked the earth to restore truth and dharma. As a young boy not yet 16 years old, he ponders the nature of the world. Pulling back the curtain of Maya, exposing the underbelly of the psychosis of human kind, he is astonished to find that we are living in a dream world wholly divorced from reality. In the opening pages of the classic Hindu spiritual text *Yoga Vasistha*, he explains his disillusionment and his dispassion toward worldly existence to his father and his

142

guru Sri Vasistha. He does this with astonishing force and poetic beauty. This book, *Rama's Most Excellent Dispassion*, presents Rama's oration and follows with an exploration of the meaning and scope of Rama's disillusionment. Rama's dispassion is both radical and blissful. It is the agony and the ecstasy. It is a precious opportunity for the reader to unfold spiritually and swim in the ocean of love.

To review further or purchase, go to www.devipress.com or search for Ethan Walker III on Amazon®.

SOFT MOON SHINING

Poems for the Mother of the Universe

Soft Moon Shining is an invitation to step into the heart of the Divine Mother. Her perpetual dance of cosmic bliss plays out through the eons as the creation and dissolution of worlds within worlds. Yet God, in the feminine form of the Mother – as the Absolute made Immanent – is ready to shower Her love and affection on any who care to turn their gaze toward Her fiery heart.

This work of poetry is both profound and beautiful in its ability to arrest the reader's conventional mind plunging the soul into the cauldron of divine intoxication and bliss. Each poem is a meditation on the Mother of the

144

universe. Feel Her love and Her compassion as the Divine Mother hugs each reader in an embrace of timeless love.

Dance with god in the form of the Mother! Revel in the call of the infinite! Swoon with joy as the heart opens wide to the roaring river of Mother love.

To review further or purchase, go to www.devipress.com or search for Ethan Walker III on Amazon®.

SOFT MOON SHINING

My beloved Divine Mother
Dance with me
      under the soft moon shining
      in the wide-open fields
      far beyond the toil and trouble
        of my busy mind

Dance with me
  before the night grows old
      while the winds of love
      still bow the grasses
        and the coyotes cry for you
        to step their way

Dance with me my beloved
  while the Mystery's Edge
    still flirts in the shadow
    of your radiant light

DIVINE MOTHER OF THE UNIVERSE

This Is How We Love You

Poetic meditations on the Divine Mother published in 2015.

TOUCHED THE OTHER SIDE

Mother of the universe
You have conjured
This dancing ocean
Of earth and plants
And beings and stars
From your dark womb
Of formless mysteries

And you hold
The crackling thunder
Of emptiness
In your begging bowl
Of endless time

And it is you who writes
Poems of love
In letters of molten gold
In the deepest cave
Of our hearts

Your children weep with joy
At your slightest touch
Flooding the world
With the brilliant lightning
Of awareness

That it was always you
Behind the curtains
Of coming and going

Your children are bowing
So low to you Mother
That our faces
Have touched
The other side

A Cup of Tea

And Secrets for the Muse

This is the author's third book of spiritual poetry.

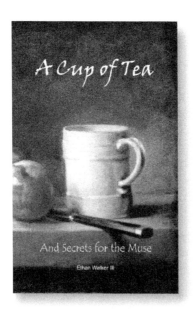

THE FIREPLACE

When the howling winds of despair
Whistle and whine
In the doorway of your life

When the cold rain of sadness
Beats against the window panes
Of your soul

Pull up a chair
And warm your hands
Gazing into the fireplace
Of your heart

Surrender yourself
To the beautiful light and love
Of your own magnificent being

Look deeply
And feel the warmth
And well-being of your heart
Filling the rivers
Of your mind and body
With ecstatic love

Experience the unfathomable beauty
That pops and crackles
In the burning embers of peace

Smile with joy
That there is so much light and love
In the fireplace of your heart

HEALTH AND HEALING AT HOME WITH ELECTRO ACUPUNCTURE

Effective Formulae You Can Use

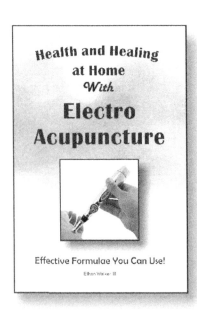

Now you can use electro acupuncture to stimulate acupuncture points in order to treat physical, mental and emotional problems. Restore balance and harmony in your body. This can be done every day in the comfort of your own home.

Traditional Chinese Medicine (TCM) is ancient – at least 5,000 years old. It is a very complex and thorough system of healing based on the view that everything in the universe is composed of pairs of opposites such as hot and cold, male and female, inner and outer and dry and wet. These pairs of opposites also compose our human bodies and are summarized in the concept of *yin* and *yang*. Also fundamental in this ancient system is the flow of a life force or life energy known as *qi* or *chi*. This is the same life force identified in Indian yogic practices and ayurvedic healing known as *prana*.

When the balance and flow of chi is disturbed in the human body, discomfort and disease are the result. We can use various acupuncture points to restore our health and well-being. This book is a catalogue of formulae designed for that purpose.

Electro Acupuncture devices are inexpensive and available on eBay® and there is a thorough discussion of the various models available.

To review further or purchase, go to www.devipress.com or search for Ethan Walker III on Amazon®.

Printed in Great Britain
by Amazon

28932013R00089